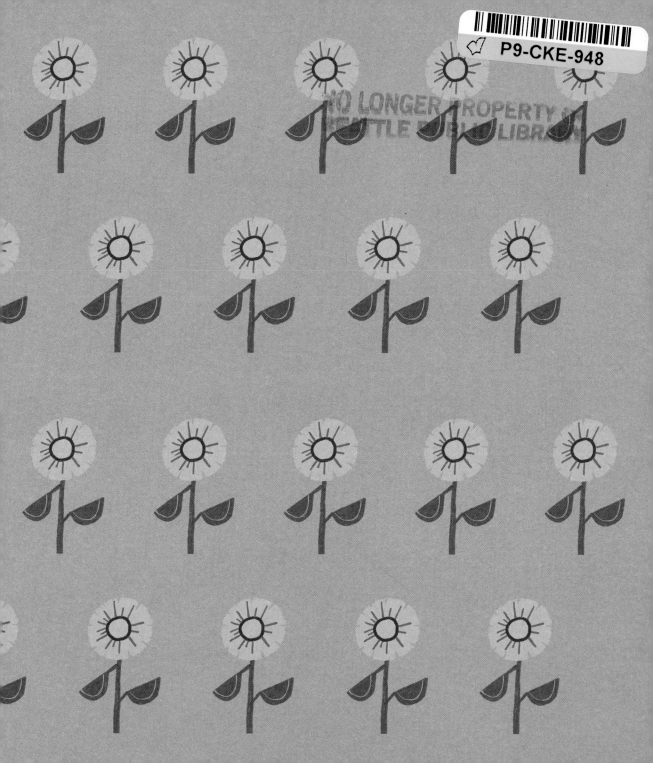

P9-CKE-948

THE
LEAGUE OF
EXTRAORDINARILY
FUNNY
WOMEN

THE LEAGUE OF EXTRAORDINARILY FUNNY WOMEN

50 TRAILBLAZERS OF COMEDY

Sheila Moeschen

ILLUSTRATED BY ANNE BENTLEY

RUNNING PRESS

PHILADELPHIA

Running Press
Hachette Book Group
1290 Avenue of the Americas, New York, NY 10104
www.runningpress.com
@Running_Press

Printed in China

First Edition: April 2019

Published by Running Press, an imprint of Perseus Books, LLC, a subsidiary of Hachette Book Group, Inc. The Running Press name and logo is a trademark of the Hachette Book Group.

The Hachette Speakers Bureau provides a wide range of authors for speaking events. To find out more, go to www.hachettespeakersbureau.com or call (866) 376-6591.

The publisher is not responsible for websites (or their content) that are not owned by the publisher.

Print book cover and interior design by Frances J. Soo Ping Chow

Library of Congress Control Number: 2018955314

ISBNs: 978-0-7624-6664-1 (hardcover),
978-0-7624-6662-7 (ebook)

RRD-S

10 9 8 7 6 5 4 3 2 1

FOR ELISE,
WHO WAS ALWAYS
LAUGHING
AND IS SOMEWHERE
LAUGHING STILL.

CONTENTS

Magnificent, Marvelous, Mighty Misfits . . . 132

Brave, Bold, Brazen Badasses . . . 182

THE LEAGUE OF EXTRAORDINARILY FUNNY WOMEN

50 TRAILBLAZERS OF COMEDY

INTRODUCTION

The *El Paso Herald* was the first to break the happy news in 1916: "Women's Sense of Humor is Steadily Developing" ran the chipper headline. What a relief! No doubt there were women all over the country, speaking to one another in worried whispers over cups of tea and cucumber sandwiches: "I don't know, Gertrude. I can't seem to manage more than a smirk. A chuckle feels positively daunting! Maybe I should *fake* it." Gasps and pearl-clutching. Heavens!

As the writer of the *Herald* article so helpfully pointed out, it appeared that more and more women were allowing themselves to enjoy their sense of humor and even participate in comedy. When they gather together, claimed the writer, they aren't just complaining about their difficult lives running households for indifferent husbands, managing ungrateful children, and dealing with the occasional freeloading relative. Instead, they *joke* about their miserable existences full of drudgery. Progress!

People seemed to fall into two camps. The first, that women were not funny, were not equipped to "get" humor or be humorous (you know, because of our small brains and delicate sensibilities). Or they fell into the other camp, claiming, "Malarkey!," "Nope!," and "Are you out of your damn mind?!" In another article published in the *Indianapolis Journal* in 1900, an anonymous writer clocking in for Team Women-Are-Funny wrote, "The claim that all wit and humor is an excessive masculine possession will not stand, and it is time it were dropped." Adding, "If women do not laugh at men's jokes it is because they are poor in quality."

More than a century later, I can still feel the heat from that burn. Attempting to defend women's equal right to create and enjoy all things funny or to have to explain why the whole "Are women funny?" debate is bananas and very last week's tweet. We're here, we're hilarious, get used to it! It's time to turn our focus to celebrating and amplifying the voices and contributions of women past and present using their humor to make the world a better, and definitely a funnier, place. Enter the ladies of *The League of Extraordinarily Funny Women*!

This project comes out of a long, genuine, personal love and passion for comedy, as both a proud comedy nerd and the kind of woman who rarely passes up an opportunity to crack sarcastic quips, break the tension by doing a silly accent, or essentially use the world as her personal funny playground. I know that humor does much more than entertain. It heals, it exposes truths, it allows us to talk about hard, difficult, and painful experiences, and it unites. Humor is powerful mojo and when it's in the hands of women—watch out.

Historically, funny women have often been overshadowed by funny men or simply obscured by a narrow focus of what comedy *should* look like. Moms Mabley might have been one of the first women performing stand-up comedy in the 1920s, but she arrived onstage carrying a legacy of funny women who came before her for decades—writing, performing in theater, vaudeville, burlesque, and even film. As I learned more about the earliest funny women, like nineteenth-century satirical writer Fanny Fern and the cheeky, outrageous vaudeville comic Marie Dressler, I knew that I wanted to compile what would be a compendium of women, comic styles, and sensibilities that spanned from the past to the evolving present. I wanted to spotlight the astonishing body of work generated by funny women as well as the ways in which each one has made important changes to both the comedy industry and the world at large.

Many women in this book are "the first" in some respect (the first African-American woman to host a late-night show, the first head writer of a major sketch comedy show on network television), but none could have made it to bat without another woman's efforts laying the groundwork before her—shifting the makeup of a writers' room, refusing to settle for less than what she was worth, standing her ground when a producer or executive said, "Women don't" or "Women can't." It takes a village to raise a planet of funny women and the women you'll meet in these pages are some of the fiercest and most fearless comedy matrons and mentors of the tribe. There are plenty of familiar faces in *The League*—women you might have admired for ages, like Carol Burnett, Gilda Radner, and Amy Poehler. But you'll also find others, like Lena Waithe, Ilana Glazer and Abbi Jacobson, and Issa Rae, who, I hope, will become your new funny lady crushes.

Choosing only fifty women to include was no small feat. I desperately wanted to go Oprah on this book: "*You* get a spot in the book! And *you* get a spot in the book! EVERYBODY GETS A SPOT IN THE BOOK!" Only in a perfect publishing world. However, in each section I've included a brief list of additional funny women for readers to get to know and love. And it has to be said that, regardless of how I've categorized these women for this book, they could each claim a spot under every heading: Each has forged the way for fellow rule-breakers, boundary-pushers, and comic innovators. They do not speak for or represent all funny women, of course. Hardly! And nothing would make me happier than to hear from readers asking, "What about so and so? How come [insert name of kick-ass funny lady here] didn't make it in?" Because that would mean: sequel! Kidding (a little). It would mean that the hilarious, groundbreaking women of *The League* truly are everywhere, multiplying by the minute, changing the world bit by witty bit.

SNARKY, SASSY, SUPER SMARTIES

SAMANTHA BEE

LENA DUNHAM

ELAINE MAY

LIZZ WINSTEAD

JULIA LOUIS-DREYFUS

TINA FEY

ROBIN THEDE

NORA EPHRON

ntellect and wit make for an incendiary combination, kind of like Beyoncé showing up unannounced at Target. There is no topic too complicated or top-heavy for the smart, funny woman to skewer with her keen insight and probing curiosity. From as far back as the late 1800s, women used humor as a kind of Trojan horse to insinuate their adroit opinions and points of view in conventionally male-dominated territory. Some of the funniest and savviest voices of the nineteenth and early twentieth centuries belonged to women writing under pen names or performing satire in theater. They used humor in clever ways to comment on hot-button issues of the day, like women's suffrage, abolitionism, and politics. Remember, this was a time in America when women were viewed as pieces of lovely, childbearing furniture. The kind of woman writing satire about the double standards of marriage in 1869 was basically a witch.

Fast-forward a hundred years and the legacy of these brainy, funny women continues without a sign of slowing down. From wading into political subjects to adding more depth and complexity to the humorous portrayal of women's experiences, this group of women are bringing all their intellectual and funny muscle to make us laugh.

EXTRA EXTRAORDINAIRES: Rosie Shuster · Anne Beatts · Lindy West · Sarah Vowell · Jane Curtain · Fanny Fern · Barbara Gallagher · Carol Leifer · Merrill Markoe · Paula Poundstone · Beth Newell · Carrie Brownstein · Aubrey Plaza · Aisha Tyler · Tracee Ellis Ross · Erma Bombeck · Mary Tyler Moore · Kathryn Hahn

SAMANTHA BEE
[OCTOBER 25, 1969–]

amantha Bee is an Atomic Fireball. That's the name of the all-female sketch comedy troupe Samantha helped to build in Toronto in 1999. At the time, the Canadian-born comedian had just graduated from the University of Ottawa. She enrolled thinking she'd become a lawyer, but after taking one class in the drama department, she quickly reconsidered and changed her major to theater. Your loss, Supreme Court of Canada. After college, Samantha auditioned for every kind of acting job available—commercials, theater, television, and film—while supporting herself (barely) as a waitress. And when she wasn't hustling to get her big break, she was breaking audiences up with the insane, comedic acrobatics of the Atomic Fireballs.

For Samantha, what was really great about the Fireballs was the tight sense of community and fellowship the women fostered. They booked, promoted, and created all their original shows out of little more than their skills and an intense passion for comedy. A lot of their material came from the happenings of everyday life, especially the petty grievances, which made for some of the funniest and most relatable comedy. Working alongside similarly smart, gifted, hilarious women,

Samantha honed her deft wit and canny intellectual and feminist perspectives. This mighty combination would ultimately carry her into the top echelons of the late-night comedy show circuit as the only woman to currently host, create, and produce her own late-night comedy show, the award-winning *Full Frontal with Samantha Bee*.

Raised by her grandmother following her parents' divorce, Samantha describes herself in interviews as a relatively shy kid. This might seem like an odd characterization of a woman who decided to ditch the law library for the improv stage. If she retained any of that shyness, comedy chased it out of her, especially when she got her first big break working on the satirical news show, *The Daily Show with Jon Stewart*. There she wrote and filmed absurdly funny field reports with strangers ranging from farmers and fast food workers to politicians and pastors.

Most Canadians were unfamiliar with Jon Stewart's show. However, Samantha and her husband, Jason Jones, were avid fans. In 2003 when Samantha heard that producers were scouting in Canada for female performers, she quickly put a tape together and submitted it. Impressed with Samantha's work, the producers invited her to audition for

Stewart in New York. As soon as she got the news, she did the thing you typically only see in movies: She walked into her boss's office at the ad agency where she had been eking out an income and quit. Cue the fist-pumping Bikini Kill or Bruce Springsteen anthem of your choice.

At *The Daily Show*, Samantha embraced her role as senior female correspondent, the token female correspondent at the time.

law loophole allowing children and teenagers to work on tobacco farms to covering national politics, such as the 2004 Republican National Convention. As the show's only female correspondent—until 2008 when Kristen Schaal joined the cast—Samantha also served as the spokesperson for pressing feminist issues. Many of these involved Samantha adopting a funny, contrarian stance to skewer the absurd, typically stupid, and, at times,

"You've got to have gumption. You've got to be willing to stand up on the stage for no money for ten years."
— SAMANTHA BEE

She relished doing location stories that no one else wanted, and saw the comedy potential in everything, even if it meant flying to interview an alligator farmer in the middle of a Louisiana swamp. In her correspondent role, Samantha supplied the mock seriousness and even indignation while her subjects' honest guile provided the comedy. Her often oddball segments gave her a chance to stand out and sharpen her comic on-air persona.

Samantha's pieces steadily evolved from traveling to Kentucky to report on a labor

even a little gross, logic surrounding contentious women's issues.

For instance, in one segment she joins Stewart at the news desk to speak about a recent debate about women serving in military combat. He mentions that some people argue that women can't be protected in the military because men can't control their base, caveman urges. Samantha cheerfully, sarcastically responds that it's simply the way it is when you're any kind of woman in a man's world. Just ask any "gal reporter, lady doctor, teacherette, or aviatrix."

Stewart announced his departure from the show in 2015, leaving many to speculate that Samantha might be next in line to assume the mantle. Instead, the gig went to Trevor Noah, which made many people a touch grumpy, and rightly so. After all, wasn't it about a thousand years past time for a funny woman to rule late night? Fortunately, the TBS network swooped in and offered Samantha a deal to develop her own satirical comedy show. She readily accepted and on February 8, 2016, *Full Frontal with Samantha Bee* came charging into viewers' lives, rearranging the field of late-night comedy forever.

Formatted like *The Daily Show* (if it ain't broke, as the saying goes), *Full Frontal* tackles the news and cultural trends of the day. The show is broken up into segments that range from monologues about topical headlines to field reports and "grab bag" pieces that are a mix of both. Samantha and her cohort—Michael Rubens, Ashley Nicole Black, Allanna Harkin, and Amy Hoggart— power the show through a raw, fierce commitment to unseat and expose injustices. There are no sacred cows for the *Full Frontal* crew. Consequently, Samantha's opening editorials are often searing takedowns of nearly everything from the NRA to Facebook to sexual harassment and wage inequality to up-to-the-minute happenings in politics. Her delivery is frenetic and excoriating, like a runaway deli slicer. She stands firm behind her opinion or point of view as she fearlessly expels her thoughtful, critical rage through a ruthlessly and very funny sardonic persona. The comedy is Samantha's spoonful of sugar, making the harsh, painful, and rancorous truths easier to swallow.

In the process of realizing her vision to create a no-holds-barred type of topical comedy show, Samantha was also able to make another significant impact in the comedy industry: supporting diversity. *The Full Frontal* writing room is 50 percent female, 30 percent nonwhite, and features people who come from a wide array of comedy-writing experience, from barely none to quite a lot.

In the short time of *Full Frontal*'s existence, Samantha Bee has not just changed the way we think about and understand current events, she's proven that there is real power in using humor to fight against inequality and hypocrisy. In fact, every week Samantha proves that a woman is not only as strong, capable, and qualified to lead the fight as any man, she might just be the next hero we never even knew we needed.

LENA DUNHAM

[MAY 13, 1986–]

Humiliation is awful, but if you're Lena Dunham, it can be awfully funny.

Lena is the fearless visionary who wrote, created, and starred in the critically acclaimed HBO show, *Girls*. On the show, Lena played twentysomething Hannah Horvath, a young woman living in New York City, struggling to become a writer and struggling even harder to become herself. In the pilot episode, Lena dares audiences not to laugh at a string of Hannah's shameful and awkward missteps.

First, her parents arrive for a visit to tell her, ungraciously, over dinner they are cutting her off financially. Then she gets fired from her unpaid internship after pleading with her boss to make her position a paid one. Finally, Hannah makes one last-ditch effort to sway her parents to float her economically for a while longer. She barges into their hotel room, clutching a sad, wrinkled stack of manuscript pages, asking them to read it and reconsider. Fixing them with a wide-eyed, wholly sincere gaze, Hannah says: "I think I may be the voice of my generation. Or, at least, *a* voice of *a* generation." It's a darkly funny experience watching Hannah's cluelessness, sense of entitlement, and self-importance collide with her parents' exasperation. This is Lena

Dunham's daring comedy at its best: mining flaws, failures, epic wipeouts, and everyday humiliations for the humor underneath it all. And that makes us all feel like less of a disaster, for a little while at least.

Lena was raised among a community of artists, thinkers, and eccentric creative types, which fueled her unique outlook on the world. Her father is a painter and her mother, Laurie Simmons, is a well-known artist/photographer, whose projects involve photographing dolls and dollhouse furniture in strange and unnerving scenes. For a lot of girls, it's younger siblings ransacking their Barbie collections, not usually their mom pilfering their stuff.

Lena's earliest interest in writing and film found a natural outlet in the bohemian atmosphere of her home and family life. She brought those interests with her later on to St. Ann's, a secondary school with a strong arts culture. Before she had even graduated from high school, Lena was studying playwriting. She wrote and produced her own plays as well as trying her hand at stand-up comedy.

At Oberlin College, Lena immersed herself in writing and film. While other students made narrative films about their families or the interesting history of the town, Lena made herself and her peers the subjects of her movies. Aiming the lens at what was right in front of her, Lena used the camera to explore regular, sometimes boring or uneventful, but always a little uncomfortable, experiences, like dating or living with a roommate or girlfriend. The same kind of psychological curiosity and dry humor that Lena brought to her college films later burst into the world of *Girls*.

She took these ideas a bit further in 2009 when she wrote, directed, produced, and starred in her own independent film, *Tiny Furniture*. It's a film that introduced audiences to Lena's way of exploiting her characters' faults and deep vulnerabilities to find the ironic comedy underneath. *Tiny Furniture* not only won the Best Narrative Film Award at the annual South by Southwest music and culture festival, it led to Lena inking a deal

"The parts I enjoy playing aren't really available to me, so I have to write them."

— LENA DUNHAM

After graduation, Lena moved back home with her parents in Manhattan, took on various part-time jobs, and continued making short films and working on other creative projects. One of these was a web sitcom called *Delusional Divas* that featured Lena and two other friends as spoiled brats from the art scene doing outrageous public stunts in an attempt to get famous. Lena using humor to push the limits of unpleasantness was a bit like the comic abrasiveness of the British show *Absolutely Fabulous* fused with the uncomfortable, public absurdity of Ali G.

with HBO to produce her own series. The idea she had in mind: four young women, just out of college, gracelessly and, often embarrassingly, moving through the confusion, heartbreak, and challenges of making a life for themselves in New York City.

Girls first aired in 2012, bringing viewers fresh, unnerving female characters who were a mess of contradictions and a mess in general. Hannah and her friends—Marnie, Jessa, and Shoshanna—navigate jobs, relationships, and their friendships with one another through disquieting experiences and scenarios laced with Lena's signature bleak humor. *Girls* was also one of the first shows, run by a young woman, to take a stark and unflattering look at dating, relationships, and, more specifically, sex. The girls of *Girls* exposed the weird, empowering, sometimes unpleasant, and often mortifyingly hilarious realities of the twentysomething hookup culture.

Girls ran for six seasons (from 2012 to 2017), winning two Golden Globes, and sparking a national conversation about feminism, race, privilege, art, humor, and the creative hurricane Lena Dunham herself. She waded into the discussion in a significant way in her 2014 memoir/essay collection, *Not That Kind of Girl: A Young Woman Tells You What She's "Learned."*

Part memoir and part girl guide, *Not That Kind of Girl* is Lena at her most pointedly self-deprecating and comically honest and insightful. She leaves few stones of her own life and experiences unturned—terrible sexual encounters, an ongoing love-hate relationship with her body, and the quagmire of anxiety and neurosis she wades through on a regular basis. Deploying her deft, funny candor as she picks through the detritus thrown up on shore from the tumultuous ocean of her life, Lena manages to make herself both relatable and sympathetic. She scores the dark matter of what life brings with lashes of black humor to unapologetically announce herself as a woman who is real, complicated, and nowhere near done with her "awkward" phase.

ELAINE MAY

[APRIL 21, 1932–]

mprov comedy is risky business. You're onstage in front of an audience, sometimes alone, sometimes with a few other people, making up stories, scenes, and characters on the fly. No rehearsal, no script; there's no guarantee that anyone will laugh, clap, or even stick around long enough to see you finish your scene. It is not an art form for the timid, unadventurous, or easily cowed. Luckily, Elaine May is none of those things.

In 1948, Elaine was not your ordinary sixteen-year-old living in Los Angeles. She was married and expecting a child. Two years later, Elaine found herself a divorced single mother seeking something more beyond preparing baby formula and cutting coupons. Nineteen fifty was not exactly a "lean-in" kind of year for women. Most women were encouraged to aspire to raising children, running the home, and not complaining about doing either. Elaine's private desire to be more than a mother was bold enough without her acting on it. But "bold" was Elaine's best friend. She left her daughter in the care of her grandmother and hitchhiked from LA to Chicago to check out the University of Chicago—rumored to be a highly unconventional place, full of artists, thinkers, and creatives. The rumors were true.

To the casual onlooker, the university probably seemed like a fantastic place to chill out for a few years and grow your brain for fun. And it was a fantastic place, but there was nothing "chill" about it. There was no age requirement to get into the university, but you had to pass all fourteen of the school's egregiously difficult entrance exams. Attendance was not mandatory and all classes were discussion-based. Your grade was determined by a single year-end exam for each class, based on everything you learned, read, and talked about over the course of the year. Defusing a bomb on a runaway train hurtling toward a nuclear power plant while fighting off a pack of ninjas would have been less pressure-filled than getting in and making it through one year of the University of Chicago.

Elaine couldn't be bothered to try to get into the university by passing its Mount Everest–like entrance exams. Instead, she spent time on campus, hanging out in classes that interested her, and falling in with a group of theater nerds in the Playwrights Theater Club, an off-campus drama group learning performance through a newish technique called improvisation.

Theater was not new to Elaine; she grew up in a Jewish family who traveled around the country performing Yiddish theater. From time to time, Elaine appeared in plays with her father when she was in her toddler years. But this improv business was nothing like the plays she knew inside and out.

It's worth noting here that in 1955 improv was not yet the hot spot of funny superstars angling for TV pilots and film deals. It was more like small groups of very dedicated and serious theater types (think black turtlenecks, black-rimmed glasses, lots of name dropping of pretentious playwrights like Ibsen and Brecht) using unscripted theater games to create new types of scene work. Some of it made for rich, dramatic acting and seemed to unleash people's playful sides, leading to scenes that happened to be very funny.

The raw, unrehearsed, spontaneous, rule-bending nature of improv appealed to Elaine, who was fiercely intellectual, deeply self-possessed, and insatiably curious about people and the inner workings of their minds. Even though she wasn't enrolled at the university, Elaine had developed a reputation around campus for being something of a renegade savant. One legendary Elaine May story that made the rounds involved her sitting in on a philosophy class where she convinced everyone, including the professor, that all the men in Plato's *Symposium* were drunk. Seriously, this was what passed for a "good time" at the U of C in the 1950s. Regardless of her antics (alleged or not), the truth behind the Elaine May mystique was that she was a unique young woman, capable of leveling astute insights about art, culture, politics, and people with a laserlike precision reserved for snipers and neurosurgeons.

Elaine found an outlet for her powerful brain when she met a theater major named Mike Nichols. He was also involved in the Playwrights Theater Club, trying to turn himself into a respectable actor. At Playwrights, Elaine did a little bit of everything, from working concessions to directing, acting, and running the players through workshops and theater games. Nichols was a similarly brilliant thinker and artist. He was one of those scary-smart individuals who had been accepted to the University of Chicago at the age of fifteen and was clearly headed to making his mark on the world in an enormous way.

He and Elaine clicked on- and offstage. They were both interested in the truth, especially as it related to the inner workings of people, of what motivated individuals, and what was behind their choices. Elaine and Nichols shared a deep fascination with the experiences of everyday life that everyone encountered. They were both brilliant, and they were both interested in seeing how the spontaneous humor that came out of real, unscripted moments onstage could reveal deeper insights into human nature. For Elaine May, this was definitely what passed as a "good time" at the University of Chicago.

Elaine and Nichols began performing together at the Playwrights Theater Club, which eventually dissolved and reformed as the Compass Players. Their chemistry was indisputable and their improvised scenes pushed modern humor in a new direction— one where the honest, sometimes terrifying reality and authenticity of a scene produced the laughs, not obvious jokes or clever word-play. It was humor for the thinking masses and it would be the driving force behind everything Elaine accomplished as an actor, director, and successful comedy writer.

In 1958 Elaine and Nichols took their brand of improvised scene work to New York to develop their own two-person shows, billed as Nichols and May. They signed with a well-known show business agent named Jack Rollins and began performing throughout the city. Audiences could tell they were witnessing something wholly original, and they were

hooked. After all, this was still a golden era of American humor, when popular comedians relied on telling jokes, delivering funny anecdotes, or skewering stereotypes in a humorous way. Nichols and May dispensed with all of that to create scenes or short sketches. They built a fully realized, miniature world onstage and invited audiences to step inside with them.

Working alongside Nichols, Elaine did more than just break ground on a new kind of comic sensibility, she also presented a different type of funny woman—smart, complicated, and equal to any man. She played doctors, lawyers, mothers, spies, analysts, girlfriends, and bankers. She played figures who had psychological depth and complexity, which is where so much of her comedy came from. Elaine let her characters be flawed, fallible, and even contentious; they were relatable, especially to women who saw themselves in these shows.

Nichols and May performed to tremendous acclaim for several years. Their Broadway show, *An Evening with Mike Nichols and Elaine May,* became a comedy album that won a Grammy for Outstanding Comedy Album in 1960. In 1962 they were invited to perform for President John F. Kennedy's birthday, the same evening that included a history-making birthday serenade by Marilyn Monroe. The duo had officially peaked. Nichols was more than happy to keep performing their act; Elaine was ready for new challenges and the two agreed to part ways to pursue other opportunities. For Nichols, that meant directing (*The Graduate*, *Silkwood*, *Who's Afraid of Virginia Woolf?*, and a ton of other award-winning movies). Elaine poured her energies

The Heartbreak Kid in 1972, based on a play by Neil Simon, and in subsequent decades brought her writing prowess to bear on a number of screenplays for successful films, such as *Reds* (1981), *Primary Colors* (1998), and the comedy smash hits *Tootsie* (1982) and *The Birdcage* (1996). Elaine has also continued to act, appearing in various films and even reuniting with Nichols in 1980 for a stage production of *Who's Afraid of Virginia Woolf?*

"The only safe thing is to take a chance."
— ELAINE MAY

into writing, focusing her formidable creative skills and shrewd comic perspectives on making films and penning screenplays.

One of her first successes came with the film *A New Leaf* (1971), a movie she not only wrote, but directed and starred in opposite Walter Matthau. Elaine was already well-known in Hollywood and show business, and the film established her as a talented screenwriter and a pioneer as a female director in a male-dominated field. She went on to direct

Elaine May remains one of the most influential, fascinating, and complicated funny women; she became an icon and a role model for generations of women working in entertainment. Elaine changed the course of women in comedy forever by doing things in her own uncompromising way, which meant breaking rules, taking risks, and exposing raw truths about our fears, sorrows, joys, and desires to find the laughter that connects us all.

LIZZ WINSTEAD

[AUGUST 5, 1961–]

In typical show business lore, the powerful male director, agent, or producer discovers a young woman singing karaoke in a bar and signs her to a recording contract or casts the actress he saw in a car commercial in his next summer blockbuster flick. Lizz Winstead put an awesome and satisfying twist on that story when she plucked a then-unknown comedian and improviser named Stephen Colbert from his job at the morning infotainment show, *Good Morning America,* in 1997 to join the cast of a satirical news show: *The Daily Show.* The move helped to propel Colbert's career, eventually leading to his own political parody show, the award-winning *Colbert Report.* While in 1997 Colbert was just another struggling comedian, Lizz Winstead was already a powerful figure and voice in comedy. She was more than just another producer or executive sent to scout talent for a show, she *was* the show—the head writer and cofounder of a comedy news program unlike anything on television to date.

Lizz Winstead traveled a long road with less than five-star accommodations on her way from unknown stand-up comedian from Minnesota to becoming a media critic and political humorist extraordinaire. As a young person, Lizz drifted through a random assortment of classes at the University of Minnesota. Lizz didn't have a clear sense of what kind of career she might pursue, only that at some point she'd find herself in New York City doing it. What guidance counselor wouldn't back this plan? A friend suggested that she should try stand-up comedy. This sounds like the same kind of friend who encourages you to try skydiving or commit light treason. However, in this case, Lizz's friend was onto something. Lizz performed her first open-mic at a local club in December 1983 and realized that this comedy stuff was it—*this* was what she was going to do in New York some day.

Lizz dropped out of college and spent the next five years perfecting her act on the Minneapolis comedy scene. Feeling ready to hit the showbiz metropolis, Lizz finally did head to New York, where she became a fixture on the stand-up comedy club circuit. Her stand-up work steadily developed, but her one-woman show, performed in 1993, altered the course of her career and television history forever.

The idea for the show came to her three years earlier during the height of America's Gulf War. While on a date at a sports bar, Lizz noticed that all the televisions were tuned to CNN; all the patrons in the place had their eyes glued to the screens. To Lizz, the footage didn't feel like reporting; it felt like watching an unending trailer for a blockbuster action film. Lizz's brain lit up as she realized she could use her humor to explore the deeper, more complicated questions about what the media and news were doing at this time.

A few years later she put together a stage show with a set that consisted of a replica of her favorite writing chair and a television. Each night, Lizz played to a crowd of three hundred people in the theater, appearing onstage in her pajamas, settling into her chair, and turning on the television to one of the major news stations covering the war. Over the course of the performance, she and the audience watched the war channel while Lizz provided savagely witty, pointed commentary about what was unfolding on the screen. It was a new beginning in her career that would permanently disrupt politics, media, and comedy.

In 1995, Lizz got the chance to pitch the executives at Comedy Central her idea for a regular comedy series. They weren't sold on the pitch she gave, but they knew the kind of smart, political humor that Lizz did best from her live shows and from her work as a segment producer on *The Jon Stewart Show*.

They proposed that Lizz develop a show poking fun at the news. In a way it would be a wider offering of the type of material Lizz had been writing and performing for years. Essentially, it was Lizz's dream job and we can only imagine that she said something to the effect of yes-absolutely-I-am-already-writing-the-first-show-as-we-speak; this was without a doubt her jam.

She teamed up with her friend Madeleine Smithberg (who was a producer at *Jon Stewart* as well as for *Late Night with David Letterman*) to create a show that was not just going to parody newscasts or the bloviating anchors from morning talk shows. Lizz's vision was for a program that looked and felt and treated itself like a legitimate news show, all the while functioning as a comedy show.

This was uncharted territory for Lizz and everyone on the show—the team of writers and producers, the cast and crew, and even the viewers. The result of this Frankenstein comedy monster was *The Daily Show*, which premiered on Comedy Central on July 22, 1996, hosted by comedian and *SportsCenter* coanchor Craig Kilborn. *The Daily Show* was formatted to open with a segment on news headlines, delivered by Kilborn from the anchor desk, followed by mockumentary-style field reports as well as celebrity interviews and debates with the show's regular correspondents. In addition to being the show's head writer, Lizz sporadically appeared as an on-air correspondent. In front of the camera, Lizz rocked the same kind of sophisticated, thinking-girl's funny she brought to the show's scripts.

In the two years that Lizz developed the show, she gifted viewers with many hilarious mainstays. The most notable ones included the cast of correspondents that grew to include Stephen Colbert, whose arch delivery and natural inclination to personify the guise of a cocky, ignorant journalist he later took to *The Colbert Report*. It also gave audiences hilariously rancorous comic Lewis Black, and the razor-sharp humor of Samantha Bee, Kristen Schaal, and John Oliver.

After parting ways with *The Daily Show* in 1998, Lizz continued taking on projects that enabled her to deploy her unique blend of intelligence, humor, and even activism. In 2003 she cofounded Air America Radio, a liberal talk radio network, with then-comedian Al Franken. The network was a little like *The Daily Show* without any of the satire. The programming included news, comedy, editorials, and interviews. Lizz cohosted the midmorning program *Unfiltered*, along with Chuck D from the rap group Public Enemy and an obscure journalist, named Rachel Maddow, Lizz had discovered at a small local radio station in Massachusetts. Those who say lightning doesn't strike twice obviously never met Lizz Winstead.

Returning to her roots as a live performer, in 2007 Lizz used her considerable political and comic firepower to put on a live show in New York called *Shoot the Messenger*. It ran as a fast-paced topical news show, lampooning breaking news as well as the parade of insipid, cartoonish morning show anchors and personalities. She later collected her thoughts and personal experiences with comedy, politics, and forging her own path in the comedy industry in a book of essays titled *Lizz Free or Die* in 2012.

Around this same time a new political cause found Lizz—the fight for women's reproductive rights. Inspired to help support women fighting for access to affordable, safe health care, Lizz decided to roll fund-raisers for Planned Parenthood into a series of stops on a comedy tour from Minneapolis to New York. The positive response floored Lizz—she raised more than $2 million and prompted a documentary film about the tour.

Lizz realized that she had a new outlet to pour her singular brand of comedy critique or "laughtavism" into. She continued to do fund-raisers, but expanded her efforts to combat what she saw as an assault on women to create Lady Parts Justice (LPJ) in 2012. Lizz and the rest of the Lady Parts Justice crew churn out all kinds of strategic and educational content in films, podcasts, live shows, and apps meant to fight for reproductive rights the only way Lizz Winstead knows how: with comedy.

"My curiosity is not a choice. It's always been a part of me. I think of it as a vital organ."

—LIZZ WINSTEAD

JULIA
LOUIS-DREYFUS

[JANUARY 13, 1961–]

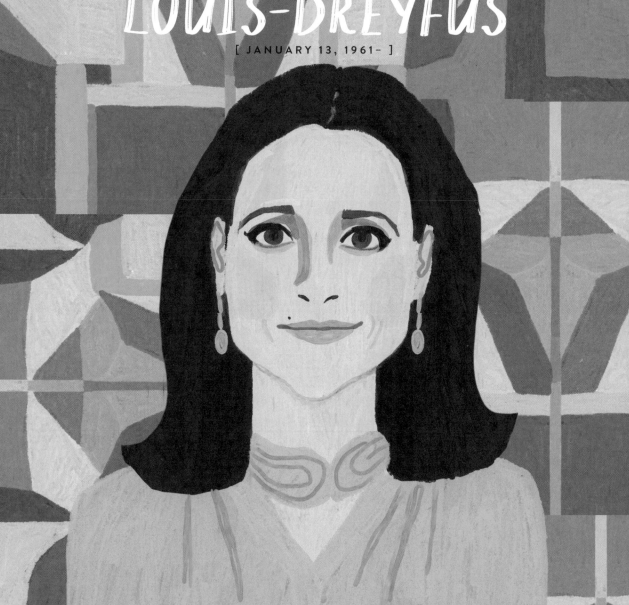

At twenty-one, Julia Louis-Dreyfus was the youngest female performer on *Saturday Night Live* in the show's history. Like so many other comedians and writers before her, Julia dreamed of joining the ranks of her comedy heroes—Gilda Radner, Jane Curtin, Laraine Newman—to make her own mark on one of America's most famous sketch comedy shows. It was something of a Cinderella moment for her. Julia was performing with Second City, the historic Chicago improv and sketch theater, while finishing up her undergraduate degree at Northwestern University when the show's then-producer, Dick Ebersol, saw her in a show and hired her along with the entire cast on the spot. Now *that's* how "happily ever after" should start.

Unfortunately, Julia's *SNL* fairy tale ended up being more like a Michael Bay disaster flick. Julia's years in the cast spanned 1982 to 1985, when the show was experiencing its own share of growing pains. During this time, Lorne Michaels, the show's original producer, had parted ways with the show and the network (he would later come back). A whole new team of network executives and production staff were doing their best (or worst, some would argue) to breathe new energy into the show. Julia struggled to fit in with the highly competitive nature of the cast and writing teams; she barely got any of her own sketches to air, and she played largely forgettable parts in the sketches she was cast in. Fortunately, it wasn't a total wash for Julia.

She met a wry, cynical comic writer who was having a similarly terrible time on the show, trying and failing spectacularly to get his sketches to air—the writer Larry David. The two became good friends, remaining in touch after their time on the show ended and they each went their separate ways. For Julia, that meant settling in Los Angeles with her new husband, Brad Hall (whom she had also met while at *SNL*), while working on all kinds of television and independent film projects.

In 1989 Julia got a call from David asking her to read for a part in a sitcom pilot he was developing with stand-up comedian Jerry Seinfeld. The character was Elaine Benes, Jerry's ex-girlfriend, and one of the quirky, funny characters rounding out the rest of the mildly dysfunctional *Seinfeld* ensemble of George Costanza (played by Jason Alexander), Jerry Seinfeld (played by Jerry Seinfeld), and Cosmo Kramer (played by Michael Richards). Julia and Jerry immediately clicked; her understated comic delivery, couched in authenticity, bore similarities to Elaine May's. She was their funny "it" girl. And before long audiences had a new hilariously feisty, feminist heroine to laugh with each week.

Driven by Julia's comic sensibilities, Elaine Benes was played as one of the boys, but she was also unapologetically her own woman. She was smart and opinionated and sometimes uncompromising to a fault. Most importantly, she was truly part of the *Seinfeld* ensemble. Unlike other female sitcom figures, cast as either a loopy or uptight foil for her comic male partner, Julia's Elaine was an equal. In one of the show's most popular and unforgettable episodes called "The Contest," Jerry, George, and Kramer make a bet to see who can go the longest without taking care of their own "business" in a sexual relief kind of way. As they are discussing it at their regular diner hangout, Elaine pipes up and says she wants in on the bet, too. At first the boys protest, but only a little bit and only because they are afraid it will be much easier for her to hold out. The episode aired in 1992 when network television more closely resembled the benign teacup ride at Disney World than the four-hundred-foot, eighty-mph, twisty, fireball death-coaster theme park ride that it is today. In other words, for Seinfeld and David

to write an episode about masturbation was a big deal—to include Elaine as a woman proud to admit she did it, too, was momentous.

Julia went on to win a slew of awards for her portrayal of Elaine, including a Golden Globe, two Screen Actors Guild Awards, five American Comedy Awards, and an Emmy for Outstanding Supporting Actress in a Comedy Series. That's some serious hardware, a collection she would only add to in the coming years. When the show ended in 1998, Julia continued to work in film and television, eventually returning to the small screen to star in a sitcom titled *The New Adventures of Old Christine*.

That show was much more conventional than *Seinfeld*, with Julia playing a single mom, raising her family, and running an athletic club. In many ways, her witty, independent character followed in the tradition of women like Mary Tyler Moore (*The Mary Tyler Moore Show*) and Bea Arthur (*Maude*), giving us comic female characters whose exploits drive the story lines. *Old Christine* ran for five seasons and earned Julia a bunch of awards, proving that she had more than one groundbreaking character in her. Two years later, Julia gave audiences a reason to actually *want* to talk about politics, with her character, Vice President of the United States Selina Meyer, on HBO's dark comedy, *Veep*.

In the role of Selina, Julia unleashes an extremely ambitious, self-involved, morally flexible, sardonic vice president desperately trying to put herself one power grab away from assuming the highest office in the country. As a woman in the cutthroat, male-dominated world of American politics, Selina is the kind of character who openly plays the system to try to beat the boys' club at its own game. Selina might be a stereotypical shrewish type of female character if she were played by anyone other than Julia Louis-Dreyfus.

Instead, Julia turns Selina into a hapless, frustrated woman, seemingly always destined to come in second place or not at all. Even when Selina wins, she somehow manages to lose somewhere along the way, usually ungracefully, often in a humiliatingly spectacular fashion. This is one of the things that makes her treacherous climb up the political ladder so funny and so much fun to watch. And it's only the latest character—one in a line that continues to stretch forward—Julia has taken on that raises the game for finding new ways to bring sophisticated, nuanced comic female characters to life.

"Have fun at all costs."
—JULIA LOUIS-DREYFUS

TINA FEY

[MAY 18, 1970–]

After more than twenty years, there was a new sheriff in the writers' room at *Saturday Night Live*. She rode into town packing her searing wit, her expansive, funny brain, and a few fart jokes because, well, the writers' room had been overrun with boys for what seemed like an eternity; she knew that change takes time and sometimes, when all else fails, a well-timed fart joke is going to be the thing to win them over. All of this to say that Tina Fey was ready to step into the role she had been preparing for her entire life: the first female head writer at *Saturday Night Live*.

Comedy was a constant fixture in the Fey household. Her parents unknowingly gave Tina an early comedy education, screening Monty Python and Mel Brooks movies and watching reruns of the 1950s hit television show, *The Honeymooners*, with Audrey Meadows and Jackie Gleason. By high school, Tina knew that humor was her strong suit. She joined the drama club and choir, and in a move that offered a glimpse of her mighty humor writing prowess, Tina penned a satirical column for the school newspaper, *The Acorn*, under the pseudonym The Colonel.

After graduating from the University of Virginia with a degree in playwriting and act-ing, Tina knew there was really only one place for her to go: Chicago, or more specifically, the improv and sketch comedy Valhalla that is Second City. Since the age of eleven, Tina had known about the hallowed halls of Second City. It was where some of her favorite comedians, like Catherine O'Hara and Andrea Martin, had trained to eventually make it on to television in the sketch show, *SCTV* (Second City Television).

If you want to join the circus, you don't sit in your bedroom teaching your hamsters how to jump through little flaming hoops (though, to be fair, I would totally watch that circus). You pack your bags and show up at the big tent, ready to get in on the action. Tina made a beeline for the center ring.

In Chicago, Tina was like some kind of comedy superhero: By day she worked as a receptionist at a YMCA in Evanston, a suburb minutes from Chicago and the home of Northwestern University, and by night, she unleashed her humor at Second City, studying improv and sketch writing, surrounded by a hilarious cohort of people. Many of these people, like Amy Sedaris and Stephen Colbert, stood out as comic geniuses seconds away from achieving massive success. Others, like Rachel Dratch and Amy Poehler, were, like Tina, driven, passionate, wickedly talented and funny women slowly advancing toward comedy greatness one laugh at a time.

Before long, Tina landed a spot in the Second City touring company. After paying her dues on the road, she auditioned and was cast in the main stage troupe. While in the cast, Tina went on to cowrite and perform in two Second City revues—shows where the sketches are connected by a common theme. The first was titled *Citizen Gates* and was exceptional not just for Tina's work as a writer and performer, but because it was the first-ever gender-equal revue cast in the theater's history. Even at Second City, Tina was cresting a wave of change for women in comedy that she would help propel into a tsunami.

For Tina, going to work at *SNL* probably seemed like a matter of "when," not "if." The time for her came in 1997 when Adam McKay, the show's then–head writer and fellow Second City alum, encouraged Tina to submit a packet of scripts to the show. Lorne Michaels liked what he read and invited Tina for a meeting. This sounds like something breezy happening over coffee and scones, but given that this was the person holding Tina's comedy dream in his hands, it was most certainly a lot more stressful and likely did not include scones. We'll never know what was said behind closed doors, but we know what ultimately happened: Tina got offered a job as one of the show's newest writers, cementing a few more stepping-stones on Tina's path to world comedy domination.

Two years later, Tina assumed the job of first female head writer for the show after McKay stepped down. For the first time in the show's history, a woman—a clever, funny woman—was driving the overall look and feel of the material. Laughs were always the bottom line, but that didn't mean they couldn't include diverse or unusual perspectives, take creative and humorous risks, and make comedy that was silly and smart while also giving strong female comedians, such as Maya Rudolph, Amy Poehler, and Rachel Dratch, opportunities to dazzle.

As if busting up the boys' club of the *SNL* writers' room wasn't enough, Tina put another notch on her comedy belt by becoming the first woman to coanchor the Weekend Update desk with her friend and fellow Second City veteran, Amy Poehler. The pair leveled witty, cutting-edge commentary about politics, celebrities, and trending stories from their own feminist POVs. At the anchor desk, Tina and Amy created a pair of sharply funny, righteous media personas, happy to take down the powers of hypocrisy. It was the kind of comedy later echoed in the humor of Samantha Bee and Jessica Williams.

The only thing that cushioned the blow of Tina leaving *SNL* in 2006 was knowing she was already on to her next project: a network sitcom titled *30 Rock*. The show parodied the inner workings of a live, comedy sketch show, "The Girlie Show," run by the perpetually beleaguered Liz Lemon, played by Tina. In Liz first, and eventually chose to adopt children in her forties—Liz Lemon bucked many feminine stereotypes that paint women as problems to solve or projects to fix. Tina played Liz as a character who accepted herself as perpetually under construction.

30 Rock ran for seven seasons, scooping up a boatload of awards from Emmys to Golden Globes. In the midst of running her own show, Tina found time to work on a bunch of movies, such as *Mean Girls* (2004), *Date*

> "Don't waste your energy trying to change opinions. Do your thing and don't care if they like it."
>
> —TINA FEY

Lemon, Tina gave audiences a strong, mildly eccentric, but ultimately admirable feminist hero women could relate to and root for. Liz Lemon staunchly advocated for female solidarity ("I support women! I'm like a human bra!") and took great, principled pleasure in avoiding the trap of such patriarchal nonsense as Valentine's Day—a perfect day for Liz Lemon to schedule her root canal. She ran a show, owned her nerdiness, put her career *Night* (2010), and *Baby Mama* (2008), where she starred alongside Amy Poehler; write a *New York Times* best-selling essay collection, *Bossypants* (2011); and squeeze in three years of hosting the Golden Globes, also with comedy bestie Poehler. This is not the picture of a comedy superstar "having it all" as much as it's the embodiment of "doing it all as much as possible while people still remember who you are and why they should give you a job."

By 2015, Tina was ready to get back into the small screen biz with her series, *Unbreakable Kimmy Schmidt*. The series stars Ellie Kemper (*The Office*) as Kimmy Schmidt, a twenty-nine-year-old woman rescued from a doomsday cult after living in a bunker for the last fifteen years. In addition to creating the show, Tina appears in it as Dr. Andrea Bayden, Kimmy's bottle-happy psychiatrist. Nothing about any parts of the morally dubious characters in the show should be funny, and yet everything about it is when it's delivered through Tina's twisted comic lens.

"Unbreakable" is a great way to describe Tina's ongoing drive to expand the world of comedy and energize the legions of women to make their own funny voices heard and make sure they're remembered.

ROBIN THEDE

[JULY 27, 1979–]

R obin Thede already had some big shoes to fill when her father named her for his most favorite funny man—comedian Robin Williams.

Growing up near Davenport, Iowa, Robin had her sights set on entertainment, which (namesake not withstanding) made her parents apprehensive. They were well-aware of the massive challenges and difficulties faced by anyone trying to make a career in the

test-drive that outcome, however; comedy was about to ask her to the prom.

Located just outside of Chicago, Northwestern was known for its exemplary theater and communications programs that churned out alums like Julia Louis-Dreyfus and Stephen Colbert. Robin got the best of both worlds—access to premium opportunities to perform and a great education, equipping her for some other career entirely. She

"Too many writers get stuck in the trap of writing what they think is funny and not considering who they are writing it for."
—ROBIN THEDE

performing or creative arts, but this was their daughter. Robin remained determined and struck a compromise with her parents: She applied to and got accepted to Northwestern University, where she agreed to work on a "real" degree while also pursuing her passion for performance. As far as parental bargains go, this one seemed pretty reasonable. After all, ending up in a solid nine-to-five gig with a 401K and dental benefits was not the worst future. She would not get the chance to

chose a major in journalism and a minor in African-American studies. When she wasn't busy with classes for her major, Robin could be found acting or working behind the scenes in any one of the many diverse performing arts productions on campus.

As it turned out, Robin's "real" journalism degree ended up playing a big role in her even more "real" comedy career, something neither she nor her parents could have ever seen coming. But before she could put all the pieces of her quirky skill set together, Robin needed to further her comedy education. After graduation, she remained in Chicago and headed for the graduate school of comedy performing and sketch writing: Second City.

Taking classes and performing at the historic sketch comedy theater, Robin found her comedy writing voice. Her work with Second City opened doors for her to write for the Academy Awards, the BET Awards, the NAACP Awards, and for people such as Chris Rock and Kevin Hart. All her hustle paid off, and Robin landed a job as the head writer on *The Nightly Show with Larry Wilmore*—a topical news and politics talk show hosted by comedian Larry Wilmore.

Robin was the first African-American woman to hold this position on any late-night show. She found that her background in journalism and media from Northwestern gave her an edge writing comedy about the twenty-five-hour news cycle. Robin began to more fully develop and explore her unique comedic slant on news and media. Out of her own perspective, she realized that there were other stories about the same events that needed to be told—ones that belonged to other African-Americans.

Aside from special reports and one-off commentary pieces about race on shows like *The Daily Show with Jon Stewart*, Robin realized that no one was giving voice to this point of view. Two weeks after Wilmore's *Nightly Show* was canceled in 2016, Robin saw an opportunity to realize a smart, funny idea for a different kind of show and she went for it—hard.

She worked with a New York–based production company to finance her pilot concept for a weekly news-based program. The show incorporated Robin's incisive, funny commentary on trending news and also featured musical performances, sketches, and documentary-style filmed segments. With an extra assist from Chris Rock, who had become a friend and mentor, Robin shot her pilot and sold it to BET. On October 12, 2017, *The Rundown with Robin Thede* launched Robin into an elite late-night club of African-American women hosts, including Whoopi Goldberg and Wanda Sykes.

Robin's brand of news show is a fast-paced, no-holds-barred, whip-smart look at the week in pop culture and trending topics as they relate to or impact African-Americans and black culture. She peppers her rundown critique—the show's opening look at headlines and newsmakers—with humor layered with various types of jokes and satire. Robin makes it look effortless, but there is a tremendous amount of intellectual dexterity in her comedy; click away for a second and you might miss three zingers embedded in an offhand comment about Oprah's glasses. Being able to keep up with Robin's elegantly spinning mind is part of the sport of her comedy and its power.

She follows in the footsteps of many funny African-American women before her in using her comedic platform to speak truth to power about more sensitive topics, like inequality and injustice. She has also made a commitment to support and promote diverse comics: Robin's staff is made up of 70 percent women, including nonblack, white, and LGBTQ employees. Her head writer is humor writer Lauren Ashley Smith, making her the second black woman to lead a writing room on late-night TV.

Maybe at some point Robin will leave this funny business in the rearview and take that journalism degree to another level. But until that happens, we'll have to settle for more comically searing rundowns of news, pop culture, and politics, courtesy of the indomitable Robin Thede.

NORA EPHRON

[MAY 19, 1941–JUNE 26, 2012]

"Women don't write here," they told her. Can you hear the "sweetie" or "honey" just parked behind that statement? The woman in question was Nora Ephron. Just out of college in the early 1960s, Nora applied for a writing job at *Newsweek* magazine. They turned her down, citing the not-at-all-insulting-misogynistic reason that they simply didn't give writing jobs to women. But all was not completely lost for the young woman who would go on to redefine an entire and *Esquire* magazine. Several years later, she had the last laugh when she joined a group of women suing *Newsweek* for sexual discrimination in a massive class action lawsuit—the first major lawsuit of its kind that opened up a national conversation about workplace gender discrimination.

Part of Nora Ephron's story reminds me of that famous scene from the Julia Roberts movie, *Pretty Woman*. After being tearfully shamed by two snooty saleswomen at a

"Above all, be the heroine of your own life, not the victim."

— NORA EPHRON

movie genre with her intelligence and her sparkling wit, writing iconic romcoms like *When Harry Met Sally*, *Sleepless in Seattle*, and *You've Got Mail*. The *Newsweek* folks had a better offer: mail room. Not exactly a corner office with a view of Central Park.

Nora accepted the job as a way of at least getting her foot in the door. However, she quickly found out that her foot only got her about as far as her knee. Nora eventually left to work for publications that actually *did* hire women writers, such as the *New York Post* Beverly Hills boutique, Roberts's character Vivian returns later in the day, newly made-over, carrying an armload of shopping bags. Reminding the women that they were rude to her and that they work on commission, Julia smiles sweetly and says, "Big mistake. Huge!" Are you getting this *Newsweek*? You let a literary sharpshooter slip through your fingers. Big mistake. Huge!

Writing was knit into the fabric of Nora's upbringing. She was raised in California by parents, Henry and Phoebe, who wrote for stage and film. One of their best-known screenplays was the 1957 romcom, *Desk Set*, starring Katharine Hepburn and Spencer Tracy. As a high school student in Beverly Hills, Nora dreamed of moving to New York to become the next Dorothy Parker, the famous American writer, satirist, and cultural critic. Creeping eastward after graduating from high school, Nora attended Wellesley College, the elite, all-women's liberal arts school in Massachusetts responsible for turning out slackers like Madeleine Albright, Diane Sawyer, and Hillary Rodham Clinton.

She earned a political science degree in 1962 and moved to Washington, DC to briefly intern at the White House during the Kennedy administration. Though there is zero chance that interning for President Kennedy is where Nora got the idea for *When Harry Met Sally*, it's highly likely that her first-hand exposure to politics and the culture of the 1960s shaped the kind of witty, insightful, high-caliber prose that made her one of America's most beloved and respected humor writers.

After leaving *Newsweek*, Nora contributed pieces to various publications when a satirical piece she wrote about the *New York Post* made its way to the paper's editor. He thought Nora was bold, refreshingly savvy, and definitely very funny. He hired her immediately. (See *Newsweek*? See how easy that could have been?) She was only twenty-two.

Nora spent the better chunk of the 1960s and '70s churning out honest, scathingly humorous essays for the *Post* as well as for publications such as *Esquire* and *Cosmopolitan*. She wrote on everything from the Beatles and Bob Dylan to national politics, fashion trends, and women's issues. Nora stood in solidarity with women on many topics, but she was not afraid of using her sharp wit and observations to criticize politics and institutions that were supposed to benefit women.

In one piece, Nora wrote about Wellesley College and how it unleashed a generation of "docile and unadventurous women." In another article, she took aim at a silly feud between Betty Friedan, author of the seminal feminist work *The Feminine Mystique*, and activist/second wave feminist icon, Gloria Steinem; and she almost caused a lawsuit at *Cosmopolitan* for a snarky satire she wrote about the fashion bible, *Women's Wear Daily*. Turns out the pen is mightier *and* funnier than the sword.

But Nora wasn't the kind of writer who

used her humor to wound. She had an innate, thoughtful curiosity about the world and our relationships that she looked at with truth and candor through the lens of humor. This included the writing she did about herself. Over the course of her long career, Nora released several essay collections—*Crazy Salad: Some Things about Women* (1975) and *I Feel Bad about My Neck: And Other Thoughts on Being a Woman* (2006)—where she unflinchingly and laughingly reversed her satirical gaze to look at herself and the sum of the good, bad, ugly, and jury's-still-out experiences of being a woman.

In 1976 Nora stumbled into screenwriting. By this time, she was married to Carl Bernstein, the famous *Washington Post* reporter responsible for helping to break the Watergate scandal. The two collaborated on a script about Bernstein's experiences that was ultimately rejected. However, another Hollywood executive had seen it and offered her a job writing—in Nora's words—a "horrible television movie." She not only enjoyed doing that, but found she had a talent for writing for the camera. Over the course of the next decade, Nora steadily racked up screenwriting credits until 1989, when she wrote a script about two best friends trying not to fall in love

with each other, titled *When Harry Met Sally*.

Starring comedian Billy Crystal and actress Meg Ryan as the pair of unlikely besties fumbling toward romance, the characters of *When Harry Met Sally* were individuals audiences recognized as any number of lovable, flawed people in their own lives. Deploying her signature droll perceptiveness about dating and relationships, Nora shattered the stereotype of the vapid, simpering, silly female romantic lead, desperately searching for love. Instead, she crafted strong, unforgettable female characters equal to men, such as Sally's best friend, Marie, played by Carrie Fisher. Marie hides her hopefulness under caustic sarcasm. She's wryly world- and romance-weary, but also vulnerable, sympathetic, and highly relatable. Marie, like so many of Nora's film females, is every woman holding out a shard of optimism that there is someone who is just as weird and messy and inexplicable as she is and who will love her anyway.

Audiences rooted for Harry and Sally as well as for all the romantic couples in Nora's films that followed—*Sleepless in Seattle*, *You've Got Mail*, *Michael*, and *Julie and Julia*. It wasn't just the happy relationships that Nora gave her audiences at the end of her

SNARKY, SASSY, SUPER SMARTIES

movies that resonated with people; it was the road she took audiences down on the way to "happily ever after"—littered with funny obstacles true to real life—that made people reflect and relate while they also laughed.

In 2012 Nora lost her battle with acute myeloid leukemia, but not before publishing *I Remember Nothing* (2010), where she deployed her signature humorous candor and sharply funny perspective to reflect on the small absurdities of life that, in the end, are where the deepest laughs lie.

COURAGEOUS, CREATIVE, CHARACTER COMICS

MOLLY SHANNON

CAROL BURNETT

AMY POEHLER

MABEL NORMAND

LILY TOMLIN

WHOOPI GOLDBERG

KATE McKINNON

LUCILLE BALL

GILDA RADNER

L ike comedy chameleons, these women seamlessly morph into old men, young pop stars, little girls, nerdy teens, first ladies, talk show hosts, political icons, sassy grandmothers, the occasional talking bear, and so many more. Wigs, prosthetic noses, prop glasses, fake teeth, and outlandish costumes are like second skins. Silly accents are passports to the even sillier worlds inhabited by these women, who bring all kinds of funny characters to life. With astonishing range and incredible skill, character-driven comics are like the Olympic gymnasts of comedy—they contort themselves into different personas in the name of doing whatever it takes to create a character that is fully realized and, hopefully, utterly unforgettable. And judging from the vast array of indelible characters who have endeared fans for ages—Roseanne Roseannadanna, Mary Katherine Gallagher, Edith Ann, Leslie Knope—these women do not disappoint.

It might seem like the easiest job in the world to be able to tuck yourself behind another person—real or fictional. But the reality is that this kind of comedy requires just as much courage and creativity as any other kind of comedic art form. All your energy goes into making this figure the funniest, most believable, most memorable character you can inhabit. And if you do it really well, that character takes on a life of her own, becoming the inspiration for a future character comic in the making.

EXTRA EXTRAORDINAIRES: Rachel Dratch · Jan Hooks · Valerie Harper · Cheri Oteri · Kim Wayans · Jane Lynch · Ellie Kemper · Carol Kane · Maya Rudolph · Andrea Martin · Jennifer Coolidge · Jennifer Saunders and Joanna Lumley · Ana Gasteyer · Niecy Nash · Anjelah Johnson-Rogers · Minnie Pearl

MOLLY SHANNON

[SEPTEMBER 16, 1964–]

There's only one person who can make something as disgusting as running her fingers up under her armpits, bringing them up to her nose, and inhaling deeply both funny and weirdly lovable at the same time. That person is Molly Shannon. In October 1995, Molly's character, Mary Katherine Gallagher, came careening into audiences' living rooms from the soundstage of *Saturday Night Live*, stealing both the sketch and our hearts.

In that inaugural sketch, Mary Katherine Gallagher auditions for her Catholic school's talent show. At first she's nowhere to be found when her name is called. Then, from just off-camera, Molly calls out "Here!" Dressed in a ridiculously looking plaid Catholic school uniform with black, boxy outsize glasses and her hair pulled back by a red headband, Molly as Mary Katherine launches herself into the room. She barrels into the scene, skidding into and colliding with a bunch of metal folding chairs. Socially awkward, interminably creepy, and maniacally intense—especially when it comes to performing—Mary Katherine Gallagher is perhaps a bit of all of us trying just a little too hard for acceptance, taking ourselves a tad too seriously, and finding any excuse to give dramatic monologues from obscure made-for-TV movies. Mary Kather-ine Gallagher would become one of Molly's most popular characters, even getting her own feature film, *Superstar*.

When Mary Katherine debuted, Molly was a fairly new *SNL* cast member, playing supporting, nondescript roles in sketches. Mary Katherine was her breakout character. Molly made her more than just a rando odd-ball. She gave Mary Katherine a bizarre, quiet intensity that made her even funnier and a little menacing. Throwing herself through walls, flipping herself over tables, and sliding around on the floor became the types of signature moves associated with Mary Kath-erine's character and heralded Molly as an impressive physical comic. This put Molly in a class of funny women like Lucille Ball and Mabel Normand (the sweetheart of slapstick comedy of the silent film era), who were not above risking a broken ankle for the sake of a laugh.

There was always a bit of Mary Kath-erine Gallagher hiding inside Molly. While attending the prestigious Tisch School for the Arts at New York University, Molly looked for representation with agents and managers. On at least one occasion she was known to give them a bit of Molly Shannon "dazzle" right there in the office, belting out show tunes to let them see her chops. That is the hallmark of a funny woman who, ironically, when it comes to getting the job, does not joke around. All that separated Molly from Mary Katherine in those offices were pratfalls and the plaid Catholic schoolgirl uniform. Despite this zany approach, Molly considered herself a dramatic actress, even as she inadvertently amused people and audiences in straight roles.

After graduation, Molly moved to LA to pursue opportunities in film and television. While she worked odd jobs to pay the bills and landed small roles onscreen, Molly

raunchier version of Mary Katherine Gallagher. The pair performed together for years before Molly got hired for a short stint on the FOX sketch series *In Living Color*. This ultimately brought her back to her roots in New York City as a new cast member on *Saturday Night Live*, where she won over fans with lovably quirky characters for six straight seasons (from 1995 to 2001).

It's true that laughter is often shaped by unimaginable pain. Molly experienced this early in her life after surviving a catastrophic car accident when she was four. The accident badly injured her father, leaving him

"I had a real desire to do physical comedy in the way that boys did. I thought, God, I haven't seen girls do that—I want to do that."
—MOLLY SHANNON

enrolled in comedy classes at Second City's theater and training school in Santa Monica. There she met another performer named Rob Muir who encouraged her to explore comedy more substantially. The two developed a live comedy show called the "Rob and Molly Show," which featured a much wilder and

to walk with a limp for the rest of his life. It also, sadly, took the lives of Molly's sister and mother. Out of that horrible tragedy came Molly's ability to create characters with resilience, hope, and a kind of confidence that came less from an inflated ego and more from their effusive self-love. There was, for example, the unhinged "joyologist" Helen Madden who appeared on talk show sketches hawking her new age, self-help books. "I love it! I love it! I love it! I love it!," Helen sang as she flailed her legs in the air, flicking her feet as if they were two live wires. And then there was Sally O'Malley.

With her enormous bouffant hairdo and firecracker-red matching pant and blouse set, Sally is proud of her age: "I'm fifty!" she hollers in an abrasive, slightly Southern drawl. It's Sally's catchphrase, one that she repeatedly shouts while falling into a dramatic lunge or attempting a split. In sketches, Sally shows up to auditions unphased by the women half her age, ready to unleash her signature moves: She likes to KICK! STRETCH! AND KICK! Molly punctuates each word by flinging one of her long legs gracelessly out like a cartoon stork. Each time the moves get larger and more erratic, as Sally becomes more worked up. It's a thing of hilarious beauty to watch. Sally is simply the tough, old showbiz broad who refuses to quit and, more importantly, doesn't see any good reason she should. Here was a new breed of female character—one who was ridiculously confident and strong. Sally O'Malley was like an eccentric badass aunt who is so proud and self-possessed that you forget to be embarrassed by her.

Following her years on *SNL*, Molly has moved easily between film and television, taking on all kinds of roles—comedic and serious. For each one she brings an impish glee that character comics get when they slip inside someone else's skin. In Molly's case, it's the way that her characters quietly and humorously exploit the universal foibles we all share—our disgusting physical habits, our strange hang-ups, and even our awkward dreams—making us feel like she's the best friend we've always wanted.

CAROL BURNETT

[APRIL 26, 1933–]

Can you imagine saying "no" to *the* Carol Burnett? That's exactly the mistake CBS executives made, well, almost made, in a meeting with the soon-to-be-legendary comedian in 1967. But let's go back.

Before she was one of America's favorite funny women, Carol was like any other girl growing up in Hollywood. Following her parents' divorce, Carol moved to the West Coast, where she was raised by her grandmother, Mabel Eudora White. To stave off some of her loneliness while living with her grandmother in a boardinghouse, Carol invented an imaginary twin named "Karen." Switching her clothes and mussing up her hair, Carol attempted to fool the other boarders by dashing out one door as "Karen" and reappearing as "Carol." It was an exhausting ruse to sustain, and Carol soon let "Karen" disappear, but the game became her first foray into a world of characters dreamed up from her rich imagination.

After high school, Carol attended UCLA, where she studied journalism before switching her major to theater to learn playwriting. During her senior year, she received a gift from a good samaritan: $1,000 (a small fortune at the time). It was an interest-free loan to help Carol get to New York to chase her true dreams of being a performer. The good samaritan gave her two conditions: Repay the loan in five years and use whatever influence she gained to help other entertainers pursue their dreams along the way. She gratefully accepted and set out to make a new life in one of the greatest show business cities in the world.

Carol may have been ready for New York, but if New York was ready for Carol it didn't show it, giving her some arctic-level cold shoulder. Like so many other performers and artists, Carol struggled to make a name for herself as an entertainer. She performed in small nightclubs and cabarets, searching for that big break when, finally, a crack appeared. Carol landed a leading role in the hit Broadway musical comedy, *Once Upon a Mattress*. Her performance earned her a Tony nomination and led to a series of recurring appearances on the popular television variety show, *The Garry Moore Show*. Finally, Carol was leapfrogging her way into the hearts, minds, and funny bones of American living rooms.

CBS executives noticed this talented young performer who could sing, dance, and get laughs playing any number of funny roles in any given sketch. It was on *The Garry*

Moore Show that Carol first introduced audiences to characters like her beleaguered, put-upon cleaning woman, aka, the original Debbie Downer. They offered Carol her own weekly comedy series, which is when they made a small error that ended up being a huge gain for Carol and for the rest of us.

To most professional funny people, getting your own comedy series was almost as good as finding that kooky lamp with the

agreed to sign their contract on one condition: She wanted a clause stipulating that at any time within the first five years of her time at CBS, she could ask the network to approve thirty episodes of one-hour programming of her choice.

No doubt, this made the executives' minds crank over as they perhaps imagined Carol putting on shows from time to time like those big holiday specials with other talented

> *"When you have a dream, you've got to grab it and never let it go."*
> — CAROL BURNETT

genie inside it. And Carol was no exception. With her love for sketch and character-based comedy, she was sure she had the perfect show concept for CBS: her own weekly variety show.

Sorry, honey (we imagine the executives saying, because, after all, this was 1967 and patriarchy was very in style)—*women don't really do variety shows. That's men's funny business, sweetheart.* Again, so much patriarchy. Carol nodded and smiled while her clever, creative brain whirred—she had come this far and wasn't about to give up now. She

guest stars like Judy Garland or Lena Horne. They agreed and everyone signed. With the ink dry and everything made official, Carol announced that her first order of business was to activate her clause. She already had the perfect idea: thirty one-hour variety shows, please and thank you very much. What else could they do? They were outmaneuvered by a woman who wore hats, wigs, and faked outrageous accents for a living. It would either be an expensive mistake or an astonishing success. Eleven years, 279 episodes, and twenty-five Prime Time Emmy Awards later, those same CBS executives would brag about signing Carol Burnett to the network. But for the moment, they, along with the rest of America, would just have to tune in on September 11, 1967, to watch the premier of *The Carol Burnett Show* and see what Carol could really do.

The Carol Burnett Show was groundbreaking in several ways. Carol was the first woman to have her own weekly variety show series. Hear that? That's the sound of a gender barrier splintering apart into a zillion particles. Carol was impressed by the atmosphere of support and camaraderie she encountered working at *The Garry Moore Show*; she created the same environment for her show, casting it as a gender-balanced ensemble which, in addition to Carol, featured comics Harvey Korman, Vicki Lawrence, and Lyle Waggoner, who was eventually replaced in 1975 by frequent guest star Tim Conway.

True to the spirit of collaboration Carol had built, her cast of performers thrived as a team where they learned from and supported each other. Vicki Lawrence credited Carol with much of her success: Lawrence was an unknown and very inexperienced performer when Carol gave her a lucky break by casting Lawrence for *The Carol Burnett Show*.

Carol became a professional mentor to Lawrence, teaching her the finer points of comedy and becoming one of her lifelong friends. And Lawrence's prickly, overbearing, perpetually displeased "Mama" character, which she created for the show, got her her own spin-off sitcom, *Mama's Family*. Carol would never have a problem fulfilling her mysterious benefactor's request to help other performers over the course of her career. In fact, she formed deep friendships with other entertainers, such as Lucille Ball and Julie Andrews, both of whom appeared many times on the show and were always game to look ridiculous for their funny pal Carol.

Most importantly, Carol's show gave her free rein to create and play comic characters that demonstrated a kind of versatility unusual for women comedians. Her elderly character Stella Toddler was a smartly dressed, stooped, slow-shuffling little old lady. One crack in the sidewalk or a chair cushion that was too slippery sent Stella falling or sliding. Mrs. Wiggins became a fan favorite. As the blonde-haired, bubble-gum-snapping, inept secretary, Mrs. Wiggins displayed a maddeningly lackadaisical demeanor, despite the urgency or chaos unfolding around her—she was essentially a middle-aged slacker. Neither Stella nor Mrs.

Wiggins had much dialogue in their sketches. Everything that made these characters hilarious came through Carol's magnificent physical comedy: her facial expressions, her posture, her ability to go sprawling out on the floor, and even her choice of costumes.

"Went with the Wind" was a sketch parody of the movie *Gone with the Wind* and parodied one of the show's most historic scenes—the one where Scarlett O'Hara, nearly destitute, meets with her love interest, Rhett Butler, wearing a gown made from a pair of drapes. In Carol's version, she plays Scarlett literally wearing the drapes—a pair of heavy, velvet curtains still attached to the rod slung across Carol's shoulders. The audience laughed so long at Carol's appearance that it had to be edited down for broadcast time constraints.

Carol's show wrapped in 1979, leaving her free to pursue film as well as stage and television roles, many of which garnered her additional awards. She's written two memoirs and even realized a "fan-girl" dream of her own when she got to play a recurring character on her favorite soap opera of all time, *All My Children*. In the spring of 2018 Carol returned to television with a Netflix series, *A Little Help with Carol Burnett*. The unscripted show features Carol and other celebrity friends, such as Lisa Kudrow and Taraji P. Henson, having candid, funny conversations with kids.

Over the course of her long career as a professional funny woman, Carol demonstrated time and time again that women comedians were just as influential, successful, skilled, and hilarious as male comedians. She proved that just because a woman could make herself look ridiculous or throw herself into an outrageous situation for laughs didn't diminish her value or intelligence. That's a living legacy that will continue to thrive long after the laughter fades and the final curtain (or drapes) fall.

AMY POEHLER

[SEPTEMBER 16, 1971–]

Mention the words "improv comedy" to people and they'll react one of two ways: smiling broadly or sweating profusely (okay, sometimes both). Amy Poehler is the kind of funny woman who can't think of anything more delicious, exciting, or super-fun than getting up onstage in front of a live audience without a script or anything prepared and making up a story, scene, or character on the spot. Let me amend that: making up a *hilarious* story, scene, or character on the spot. But Amy has always known that improv is more than just performing spontaneous comedy; it's also about building trust, cultivating faith in the unknown, and taking creative risks. All of these things are elements threaded throughout Amy's journey from obscure funny girl to the humorist behind impersonations of Hillary Clinton, Kelly Ripa, Sharon Osbourne, the plucky and fierce civil servant Leslie Knope, and a slew of characters happy and completely at ease in their weirdness.

Born and raised in Newton, Massachusetts, Amy studied at Boston College, where she got her first glimpse inside the precarious world of improv while performing with the campus group My Mother's Fleabag. She took her bag of magic comedy tricks with her from Boston to Chicago—some would say the birthplace and epicenter of improv.

Amy enrolled at Second City, where she took classes and performed. It was there that she crossed paths with another talented, witty improviser named Tina Fey. Tina and Amy wound up in the same Second City touring company, traveling all over the country with a troupe of comedians in a style less like rock stars and more like a dust bowl family of seven from a John Steinbeck novel with one can of beans to share among them. The takeaway: Artists start out poor, touring is hard and often very greasy, but ultimately rewarding. The miles logged on these grueling tours—both on the bus and onstage—worked Amy's improv and comedy muscles to heavyweight-class proportions.

While immersed in the Chicago improv scene, Amy became involved with Second City's sister improv theater, ImprovOlympic (or iO), where she met a group of comedy powerhouses in the form of Matt Besser, Adam McKay, Ian Roberts, and Matt Walsh. She and Matt Besser sparked comically and romantically, and he invited her to be a part of a new performing group called the Upright Citizens Brigade (UCB). Amy's life became a buffet of performing with Second City, at iO on a team called Inside Vladimir alongside Tina, and around the city with UCB. The Citizens ultimately morphed into a core team of players, consisting of Matt Besser, Ian Roberts, Matt Walsh, and Amy. To the girl who landed her first laugh by accident as Dorothy in a fourth-grade production of *The Wizard of Oz*, performing improv nearly seven nights a week with people she respected, admired, and who made her tear up laughing, life could not possibly get any better.

Spoiler alert: Life was about to get way better!

Amy and the UCB crew decided to try their comedy luck in New York. Their eyes were set on a bigger town with a bigger goal: landing their own TV show. The quartet were completely at home with the DIY sensibility of hustling to put on shows wherever they had space and opportunity. This included public street corners, industrial lofts, and in the back of sticky, dive bars. They eventually secured a tiny, cramped, sort of skeezy theater space in Chelsea. But it was all theirs and they scrubbed floors and splattered paint on walls and loved it into existence. To make ends meet and keep the theater from getting condemned, Amy and the UCB crew taught classes. What followed from Amy's hard,

hilarious work with her funny friends were a series of breaks and lucky happenings that fell like dominoes.

Comedy Central signed the group to a television sketch comedy deal. Conan O'Brien featured them on his late-night talk show. The UCB theater outgrew its shoebox performance space and moved to a bigger location. The theater's classes and performing teams grew, attracting future famous funny people, such as Aubrey Plaza (*Parks and Recreation*), Kate McKinnon (*SNL, Ghostbusters*), and Ellie Kemper (*The Office, Unbreakable Kimmy Schmidt*). Again, Amy thought that things could not be much sweeter than getting paid to make people laugh; working with smart, funny, talented people; and growing a comedy art form she loved. And that's when life doused Amy with a monsoon of good fortune in the form of getting to audition for Lorne Michaels at *SNL*.

Amy auditioned with characters who had accents and believed in wacky ideas (America was discovered by aliens!), and she might have pulled an early version of a future sketch character—the hyperactive little girl named Kaitlyn—out of her pocket, pinballing around the stage like, well, overly stimulated Kaitlyn. Basically, at her audition, she did what

Amy does best: She showed up to play, have fun, and make people laugh. It worked. Amy started her epic tenure at *SNL* in the fall of 2001, where she charmed audiences and fans for the next eight years.

During that time, Amy not only gifted fans with unforgettable characters and impersonations, she also made history as the first woman to coanchor the Weekend Update news desk with another female cast member: Tina Fey. Together again, the two liquefied a comedy glass ceiling, rocking the update segments with smart, wry commentary on politics and pop culture served up with a feminist slant. Tina and Amy sent the world an unmistakable message: When women (especially funny women) join forces to work together and combine their gifts for the greater good, everyone wins.

Amy's playful comic confidence and willingness to make herself literally look zany, ugly, bizarre, or even rude in the name of laughter carried her beyond the *SNL* soundstage.

In 2008 she unleashed the indefatigable Pawnee Parks Department champion Leslie Knope on TV audiences. Principled to a fault, Leslie won over audiences with her stalwart defense and love of local government and breakfast food. Her character is highly competitive, insanely ambitious, and, most importantly, an enormously loyal friend. In Leslie, Amy created a funny female character who worked to make everyone else around her successful, especially her other female friends. This was a variation of a principle Amy had learned through her years of improv: Strong players make everyone around them look better. Leslie's relentlessness at seeing her friends happy and making their dreams come true added an even more powerful dimension to this strong, feminist character. And when Leslie preached female solidarity in the form of "ovaries before brovaries," you believed her.

After departing from *SNL*, Amy, like Leslie Knope, powered onward toward funny woman domination. She started her own production company. She somehow found a few minutes to host the Golden Globes with her comedy partner in crime, Tina. They were the first pair of female cohosts in the Academy's history and the pair crushed it so hard they hosted twice more. Amy took on more film roles in movies such as *Baby Mama* and *Wet Hot American Summer* and provided the voice for "Joy" in Pixar's *Inside Out*. With all her free time, she wrote a *New York Times* best-selling memoir, *Yes, Please!*, and helped found an online support and educational network for girls called Amy Poehler's Smart Girls.

And she's just getting started. Whether writing for TV, dropping in at UCB to perform, or nurturing and mentoring a new batch of extraordinarily funny women, Amy continues to inspire and empower generations of girls and women to live the fundamental improv rule of "yes, and"—to believe in themselves and trust in the thrilling unknown that makes life incredibly fulfilling and incredibly *fun*.

> *"There's power in looking silly and not caring that you do."*
> —AMY POEHLER

MABEL NORMAND

[NOVEMBER 10, 1892–FEBRUARY 23, 1930]

In 1910, there were certain things that American women simply did not do. They did not run down the street chasing after milk wagons. They did not slide down the bannisters of sweeping staircases, flashing their petticoats and lacy knickers as they tumbled head over heels to a stop. They most definitely did not attend parties where they ended up drinking too much champagne, only to become tangled up in a set of heavy drapes as they danced the night away. Absolutely no way did a woman dare to do any of these things unless, that is, that woman happened to be Mabel Normand: the star and comic sweetheart of director Mack Sennett's outrageous slapstick silent film comedies of the early 1900s.

Mabel joined the ranks of other popular silent film stars, such as Charlie Chaplin, Buster Keaton, Harold Lloyd, and Roscoe "Fatty" Arbuckle, known for their physical comedy high jinks. Audiences loved to laugh at Harold Lloyd dangling precariously from the arm of a giant clock fifty stories above the city or Fatty Arbuckle getting beaned on the head by a carnival hammer. Men were built to take such abuse. What else would explain football and hot-dog-eating contests?

Women, on the other hand, were designed with something else in mind entirely. Sure, we make and expel fully formed humans, but that little hat trick aside, women have always been perceived as the gentle, docile, demure gender. For a woman to risk her reputation and social standing by performing the kind of brash, risqué physical comedy reserved for men, she was either very brave or very ill (or a little bit of both). That's why Mabel's talents and enormous comedic success were so extraordinary: She proved that the only barriers to being a funny woman were the ones meant to break your pratfall.

Mabel grew up in Brighton, New York, where, as a teenager, she worked as a model for photographers and popular artists. Though she enjoyed modeling, Mabel was actually intent on becoming an illustrator. However, her friend, Joyce, who worked across town at Biograph Studios in the relatively new "moving picture" industry, thought Mabel was a natural for films. At first Mabel was skeptical. After all, she not only had her dreams of being an illustrator, but she also made perfectly fine money modeling. After much needling, Mabel relented and agreed to visit Joyce at the studios. There she met D. W. Griffith, a talented, young director already making a name for himself in the movies. Griffith would go on to produce several historic films that essentially changed the nature of cinema. No big deal. Griffith saw Mabel's potential as well and quickly cast her in a film. To her surprise, she found that she took to movies naturally, which changed the course of her life forever. Again, no big deal.

Though she made a few pictures with Griiffith, it wasn't until Mabel began working with Mack Sennett in 1912 that she found her niche as a comic actress. Sennett ran Keystone Films, best-known for churning out slapstick comedy capers featuring the Keystone Cops, a group of klutz-prone policemen who caught themselves on fruit carts and wagon wheels more than they caught criminals. Sennett recognized Mabel as an unusual type of comic actress; she was sweet-faced, but also feisty, self-possessed, and physically agile. In most cases, women in silent film comedies were only there to let the funny men have the spotlight and get all the laughs. These actresses might have managed some humorous reactions to the antics of their leading men—a silly wink or an exaggerated facial expression—but for the most part they were lovely foils against which the comic anarchy of the film turned. Not so with Mabel. She played just as hard as the boys for laughs, eventually coming to be known as the "female Charlie Chaplin" for her masterful control over her comic facial expressions, quirky mannerisms, and accomplished physical humor.

Mabel quickly ingratiated herself to audiences, becoming a popular silent film comic. She was the first woman credited with enduring the "pie-in-the-face" gag in the 1913 Keystone short, *The Ragtime Band*. This was a visual gag introduced in movies in 1909 by comedian Ben Turpin. Simple, dopey, and sticky, it had all the makings of a classic comedy move, which is exactly what it became. Mabel's willingness to mess up her mug for laughs showed people that there was a new way for women to be funny—by being fearless.

In the 1915 film *My Valet*, Mabel literally goes the distance for her comedy. The movie includes a scene where Mabel gets tied to a rock and cast out into the ocean by a treacherous villain (not cool, treacherous villain!). She wrestles with the current the way decades later Lucille Ball would tangle with riotous kitchen appliances or oversized costumes. The sequence works because Mabel was a strong swimmer, able to maintain control in the water in order to exaggerate the appearance of being helplessly tossed about by the waves. Aware that this was a comedy, audiences relaxed, knowing that Mabel was never in any real danger and could, instead, enjoy the spectacle of her funny war with the waves.

Far from just being a leading slapstick comic, Mabel was one of the first women behind the camera to direct comedies. By this time Mabel and Sennett had developed a romantic relationship and, in 1914, he encour-

through this company until it dissolved in 1918, leaving Mabel to return to her slapstick roots. She was signed by the Goldwyn studio, starring in shorts, similar to today's half-hour sitcoms.

Mabel's career stalled in the mid-1920s. She suffered from a number of health problems, some related to the residual effects of contracting tuberculosis as a child and oth-

> *"Of course there will always be slapstick work. That brand of humor is still popular on the stage, with some people, and there will always be more or less of a demand for this kind of fun."*
> — MABEL NORMAND

aged her to become a director. Most of these films no longer survive, but of the few that do it's apparent that Mabel was able to readily master and, in some cases improve upon, the same basic film techniques used by film impresarios like Sennett and Griffith.

Along with directing, Mabel was also one of the first female film comedians to briefly run her own film company: the Mabel Normand Feature Film Company. She starred in and produced both comic and dramatic films

ers from a rumored addiction to drugs and alcohol. Compounding things, Mabel was also linked to several high-profile criminal scandals, one of which involved the murder of director William Desmond Taylor. Mabel was the last person to see Taylor alive the night he was killed and though she was intensely interrogated by authorities, Mabel was ultimately ruled out as a suspect. Taylor's murder has gone unsolved to this day. Very *E! True Hollywood Story*. With her health in steady decline, she was unable to handle the rigors of physical comedy and Mabel faded from public life. She passed away on February 23, 1930, at the age of thirty-seven, at her home in California.

During the height of her career in the latter part of 1919 and the early 1920s, Mabel worked alongside a new vanguard of female physical comics, such as Marie Dressler and Anita Garvin who were rising through the ranks of cinema. They flourished thanks, in part, to Mabel's previous work that created more opportunities for women to perform physical comedy. Mabel's comic antics also helped make it more permissible for audiences to laugh at and enjoy watching women at the center of humorous chaos. Her astonishing body of work helped these women, and all manner of physical comedians who followed, find their own voices and styles. She leaves behind a brilliant and enduring legacy for a girl who thought she was better off drawing pictures then starring in them.

LILY TOMLIN

[SEPTEMBER 1, 1939–]

Nineteen sixty-nine had barely gotten started and there was already a lot of history being made in America. President Richard M. Nixon took the oval office, NASA launched *Apollo* spaceships to the stars in hopes of putting a man on the moon, and a wacky, socially and politically irreverent NBC sketch show called *Rowan & Martin's Laugh-In* was about to introduce audiences to one of its newest cast members: a wiry, dark-haired woman, named Lily Tomlin, with an impish face and a wry delivery.

The show's title was a riff on the "love-in, sit-in, be-in" hippie counterculture sweeping across the country in the late 1960s. These types of events were meant as peaceful protests, with people gathering to speak out against the government. They made colorful signs, gave speeches, but they did not smoke a lot of marijuana and play loud music—nope. It was a free-wheeling time in the nation's history before the country would hang a sharp right turn into a terrible war, an embarrassing presidential scandal, and an ill-advised love affair with polyester shirts. But all of this was on the horizon.

For the moment, TV viewers had a fun, hip, hot take on politics and pop culture in the form of *Laugh-In*. Performed against a backdrop of trippy, pop-art sets, the revolving cast put up fast-paced sketches, short comedy gags, and taped segments that skewered the happenings of the day. The show's format required performers to do a lot of characters, the odder or more socially bizarre, the better. For Lily, this was a made-to-order dream gig. Characters were her constant companions; she'd been hanging out with them since embarking in comedy as a stand-up performer in the early 1960s.

One of those characters to grace the *Laugh-In* soundstage was Edith Ann—a snarky five-year-old, wise beyond her years. Dressed in baggy coveralls with a patchwork smock and bright, blue blouse, Edith curls up in an oversized rocking chair. She delivers pithy monologues about her life as a little girl or about things going on in the world. Self-possessed in a way that only children can be, Edith typically ended her stories with the tagline "And that's the truth," followed by blowing a noisy, messy raspberry at the camera. Edith was a simple, sweet character who won audiences over immediately, even scoring her a guest spot on the PBS children's show *Sesame Street*. When you get to rub elbows with Big Bird and Kermit the Frog, that's when you know you've hit the big time. Though only one of many in Lily's storehouse of funny people, Edith illuminated a quality that became a hallmark of Lily's comedy: using humor and playfulness to speak hard truths.

Growing up in a working-class family in Detroit, Lily lived in a predominantly African-American neighborhood. Many of her relatives came from Appalachia, migrating from the South to Michigan, where they took industrial, blue-collar jobs and voiced strong opinions on everything from the price of milk to but not unique to Lily's family. She would later take this perspective about women's inequality to build strong, feminist characters, such as the gutsy, overqualified, undervalued, patriarchy-busting Violet Newstead in the hit movie *9 to 5,* costarring Dolly Parton and Jane Fonda.

Set on becoming a biology major, Lily enrolled at Wayne State University. But after she landed a part in a campus theater production, Lily discovered that learning about

"After all, in private we're all misfits."
—LILY TOMLIN

the latest political scandals. Lily drank it all in. She drew from the ideas, beliefs, mannerisms, and lives of these figures to shape many of her most enduring characters.

As she grew older and began to develop her comedy, Lily would also revisit and incorporate the gender politics she observed at home as a kid. In typical fashion for most households in the 1950s, Lily's mother was a stay-at-home mom while her father worked in a factory. One had a modicum of freedom and opportunity while the other did not. It was a troubling dynamic, to say the least, the wild wonders of cell division was a lot less appealing than performing onstage for laughter and applause. (Sorry, bio majors of the world; I'm sure you're all the life of the party.)

After graduation, Lily performed stand-up comedy in nightclubs around the Detroit area before moving to New York in 1962 to tackle comedy in the big city. Unfortunately for Lily, she ended up being the one who got tackled. She found out that she simply wasn't quite ready to withstand New York's ruthless performance scene. Lily took what she learned from this experience and moved back to Detroit to vigorously perfect her act. Three years later, Lily felt ready to try again. She headed back to New York, got a job as a bookkeeper at the Marvin Josephson talent agency, and took her brand of character-driven comedy, which included the sassy five-year-old Edith Ann, to every nightclub and theater that would book her.

Lily got a huge break in 1965 when she was booked to perform on the wildly popular *Merv Griffin Show*, a talk show that also featured entertainment. This boost put her on the radar of *Laugh-In* producers, who cast Lily for the show in 1969.

In addition to Edith Ann, Lily introduced several other characters, such as Susie Sorority, the obnoxious, high-strung sorority girl concerned less about real life than she was about Greek Life, and the unforgettable telephone operator Ernestine. Lily's Ernestine was a smart, chipper telephone operator who used her job to cheerfully knock the mighty and powerful, including taking comic jabs at the telephone company itself. Ernestine became one of Lily's most enduring, iconic, and widely performed characters. In 2016 Lily donned her Ernestine wig and telephone headset to film a PSA for PETA (People for the Ethical Treatment of Animals). In the spot, Ernestine sits behind a desk with a mock Sea World logo on the wall behind her depicting a blue fin shackled to a ball and chain: "This is Ernestine," she says into the mouthpiece, "returning your call from Sea World, where everybody has a whale of a time . . . except for the whales!"

Lily has gone on to have a hugely successful career in film, television, and stage comedy. She released three comedy albums in the 1970s, one of which was adapted as a live film performance titled *Lily Tomlin on Stage*. She won a Tony Award in 1985 for her performance in the one-woman hit play, *The Search for Signs of Intelligent Life in the Universe*. *Search* revolves around the perspectives of multiple characters, all played by Lily. It was written by Lily's girlfriend at the time, Jane Wagner (the pair were married in 2013 after forty-two years together), and made into a film in 1991. Her films have also given audiences stand-out characters, such as *9 to 5*'s Violet and Linnea Reese in Robert Altman's 1975 satire, *Nashville*, for which Lily earned a Best Supporting Actress Academy Award nomination.

Throughout the 1990s and into the turn of the twenty-first century, Lily has done the television equivalent of photo bombing:

showing up on a sitcom or drama in a relatively minor role and stealing the entire episode. From playing Will Truman's deliciously sardonic boss on *Will & Grace* to keeping the fictional President Bartlett on his toes as his droll presidential secretary on *The West Wing*, Lily has continued to shape authentic female characters grounded in strong perspectives that have a way of using humor as a conduit for wisdom.

One of her most recent characters is Frankie Bergenstein on the scripted comedy *Grace & Frankie*. Lily's Frankie is a lovable, crass, quirky, feminist hippie played opposite Jane Fonda's uptight, conservative, insufferable Grace. It's an odd-couple pairing that allows Lily to shine, playing a character coming to terms with aging, divorce, and dating while stubbornly refusing to change, conform, or compromise her principles. In other words, Frankie is authentic; she's a woman using humor as a weapon against a world trying to erase her and nullify her opinions. In the hands of any other actor, Frankie would be a hokey, stereotypical "senior" character, but in Lily's accomplished grip she's a hilarious, moving, smart, powerful woman with the playfulness of Edith Ann, the chutzpah of Ernestine, and the elastic, funny bones of Lily Tomlin.

WHOOPI GOLDBERG

[NOVEMBER 13, 1955–]

A throng of people clustered outside of Whoopi Goldberg's show in San Diego. Most people would have been overjoyed to see a large group of people gathered outside the club hours before they were set to perform. Except these people weren't fans; they were protestors. Let's just say that in San Diego in the early 1980s, Whoopi had earned a *reputation*. For starters, she was an African-American woman doing stand-up. At a time when female comics of all shapes, sizes, and colors were something of a growing minority, that designation alone made people sit up and talk about the young comedian.

But Whoopi (born Caryn Elaine Johnson) was also gaining notoriety for being a comic who did more than talk about airplane food or shopping malls. Whoopi's material covered all kinds of subjects that not everyone found particularly humorous, like, for instance, teenage abortion. Oops. Cue the picketers. Fortunately for the rest of us, Whoopi was not going to let a little thing like an angry mob slow her down. San Diego was just one step on an epic road that would eventually earn her a Grammy, an Emmy, an Oscar, and a Tony.

Raised in Manhattan, Whoopi developed an interest in acting when, at the age of eight, she first appeared onstage in a production by the Helena Rubinstein Children's Theater. She took her love for theater with her as a teenager, when she became a counselor at a summer camp. There she threw herself into their dramatic arts program, performing in their annual Broadway show revues. Unfortunately for Whoopi, nothing about high school or learning came easy; unbeknownst to her at the time, Whoopi was dyslexic. She dropped out and, following the breakup of her first marriage and the birth of her daughter, moved to California, eventually settling in San Diego.

In California, Whoopi began to thrive creatively. She became a founding member of the San Diego Repertory Theatre and joined an improv group called Spontaneous Combustion. Whoopi took on any job she could to make ends meet, which included becoming a beautician—in a mortuary. Take note and remember this the next time you're complaining about working at a cell phone kiosk in the mall.

Even as she enjoyed performing with her improv group, Whoopi found that when it came to moving beyond those shows, she was limited. It had less to do with her talent and more to do with a general atmosphere of social ignorance (the same atmosphere lingering around America since the Puritans landed). Bookers, directors, and promoters were simply narrow-minded when it came to seeing the potential of funny women in general and funny women of color more specifically. It was clear that if she wanted to develop her career she was going to have to take matters into her own hands; she began writing and workshopping character-based pieces for what would become her hit one-woman show, *The Spook Show.*

Even with Lily Tomlin's one-woman show and other women comics who peppered their acts with stories, there wasn't anything teenage girls from California's San Fernando Valley. Whoopi's Valley Girl giggled and flirted and tossed her imaginary perfect hair as she talked about being approached by "total hunk-olas." There was Fontaine, a hip, junky-thief with a PhD in literature from Columbia—"I got a PhD that I can't do shit with; I stay high so I don't get mad!" she says to the audience. In this section of the show, Fontaine tells the surprisingly poignant story of how visiting the Anne Frank house in Amsterdam softened her jaded perspective about life and humanity.

"I grew up in a time when it would never have occurred to anyone to tell me there was anything I couldn't do."

—WHOOPI GOLDBERG

quite like Whoopi's *Spook Show*. From the recesses of Whoopi's agile mind and through the subtle transformations of her physicality, came thirteen fully realized, racially, economically, culturally, and politically distinct characters.

There was her "Valley Girl," a goofy, pop culture stereotype in the 1980s of affluent

Whoopi also performed a disabled woman, her head tilted against her shoulder, who quips: "This is not a disco body." And she entered the world of a little black girl who fastens a white pillowcase over her hair hoping to dream it into blondeness. These were not the wacky, comedically, and physically elastic characters of Lucille Ball or Gilda Radner.

They were nuanced, sophisticated, and beautifully and humorously wrought living portraits of women who, in telling their stories, invited others to confront their own ideas about race, class, or ability. Whoopi's *Spook Show* was a masterpiece. One that no one saw for the first two days she performed it in New York City.

Whoopi was basically just one more unknown actor performing a show in one of America's most savagely competitive showbiz towns. It wasn't entirely ludicrous to think that a handful of people or less happened to be in the audience those first couple of nights. Luckily, one of those people was Mel Gussow, a critic for the *New York Times*. In the 1980s, getting a favorable print review in the *Times* was the twentieth-century equivalent of a tweet going viral. In his review, Gussow wrote:

Quickly we realize that Miss Goldberg is not simply a stand-up comedian but a satirist with a cutting edge and an actress with a wry attitude toward life and public performance.

And:

It may not be long before people will try to compare future comics to the inimitable Whoopi Goldberg.

Not long? Try about fifteen minutes.

The day after the review was published there were a lot more than a half-dozen people in the audience. And the day after that even more. One night the famed singer and actress Bette Midler was in the crowd. And another night the even more famed director, Mike Nichols, came to see this funny woman and her parade of characters. And that's when Whoopi's world turned inside out and upside down in all the best ways. Nichols offered to produce Whoopi's show, which in New York meant one thing: Broadway.

The Spook Show ran for 156 sold-out performances and put the name Whoopi Goldberg on everyone's lips, including another kind of well-known Hollywood big-shot type named Steven Spielberg. He singled out Whoopi as ideal for his next project, an adaptation of Alice Walker's novel, *The Color Purple*. One of America's most fascinating funny women was about to revisit her dramatic acting roots. *The Color Purple* was an enormous success and earned Whoopi an Oscar nomination for Best Actress. As a comic and dramatic performer, Whoopi was a double threat.

Over the course of the 1980s and '90s Whoopi appeared steadily in movies and on TV. In the 1980s, she teamed up with comedy pals Robin Williams and Billy Crystal to host Comic Relief, a series of successful fundraisers to combat homelessness. She won an Oscar for her role as Oda Mae Brown, the prickly fake psychic–turned–real psychic in 1990's *Ghost* (also known as the film starring Patrick Swayze's clay-coated abs). She charmed audiences as the feisty Vegas lounge singer hiding out from the mafia in a convent in 1992's *Sister Act*. In 1994 Whoopi became the first woman to ever host the Academy Awards and in 2001 was also the first woman honored with the prestigious Mark Twain Prize for American Humor.

When she isn't lending her massive talents to any number of film, theater, or web-based creative and performing projects, or working on behalf of human rights campaigns, Whoopi helms the daytime talk show, *The View*. Never one to hold back on her opinions—whether laced with humor and sarcasm or simply laced with the truth as she sees it—Whoopi's contributions to the show definitely help broaden and challenge everyone's "views."

Whoopi's long journey between *The Spook Show* and the Academy Awards was not easy or direct. Over and over again, she had to confront and overcome social and industry biases against being an African-American woman who earned her living making people laugh. Each time she did so by winning a new role or making a new opportunity for her brilliant, authentic characters to shine, the comedy world cracked open a little wider and then all of our worlds got a lot funnier.

KATE McKINNON

[JANUARY 6, 1984–]

There's truth in the saying that "Sometimes the best man for the job is a woman." Just ask Kate McKinnon. In the long history of *Saturday Night Live*'s outsize boys' club, she's one of *SNL*'s most gifted comic chameleons, morphing into anyone from pop star Iggy Azalea to Attorney General Jeff Sessions and all without breaking a sweat.

Take, for instance, her *SNL* commercial parody of pop star Justin Bieber for Calvin Klein underwear. Dressed as Bieber in a ribbed tank and white jockey shorts, sporting a slicked-up cropped hairdo, Kate lampoons the real ad in a series of quick cuts where she grooms nonexistent facial hair with the world's tiniest comb and sips from a child's juice box as her voice overstates: "I'm not supposed to drink, but I do." It's the kind of smart comedy that Kate has become known for in her work on *SNL*—one that passes beyond pure silliness into sly social commentary about media, celebrity, consumerism, sexuality, and, of course, humor. Admittedly, that's a lot to get out of an underwear commercial, but that's one of the things that makes Kate McKinnon stand out from the rest of the funny pack.

Kate slipped into her first character in the fifth grade. Auditioning for the highly sought-after "Queen" of her class's reading week, Kate affected a British accent to get the part. She also got laughs and grins, which put her on the path to performing comedy in earnest.

At Columbia University, Kate studied theater and cofounded Tea Party, a musical comedy group. She continued to audition for all kinds of performance work following graduation, and in 2007 was cast on Logo Network's groundbreaking, *Big Gay Sketch Show*, where she remained for three seasons.

While living in New York, Kate took classes at the legendary Upright Citizens Brigade Theater (UCB), an improv training and performance center cofounded by none other than Amy Poehler. So many gifted funny people from UCB went on to gigs at *SNL* that it was hard to imagine a world where Kate wouldn't eventually land on the show's soundstage in studio 8-H of Rockefeller Center.

Cut to Kate landing a job at *SNL*.

Hired as a featured player in 2012, Kate became a "regular performer" a year later. Along with currently being the longest-serving female performer, she is also the show's first openly lesbian cast member, a fact that means there's a chance some funny gay girl in Topeka is watching Kate each week, thinking, "Watch out, McKinnon. I'm coming up right behind you."

Kate's love for character work—*SNL* alum Molly Shannon's Mary Katherine Gallagher being one of her character crushes—amped up the rich, funny opportunities for Kate to stretch her comedy muscles and take on personas that ranged from Ed Sheeran and Keith Urban to Ruth Bader Ginsburg and, of course, the indelible Hillary Rodham Clinton.

Though the contentious 2016 American presidential election was enough to give the country a collective stomach ulcer, Hillary Clinton's candidacy gave Kate a brilliant chance to breathe new life into an impersonation recently done on the show by Amy Poehler. Kate's Hillary is deadly serious, tightly wound, ruthlessly ambitious, and yet unable to stay completely contained as a consummate professional in the wake of the election mania. In one of her most memorable sketches, Kate appeared with the real Hillary Clinton who played a bartender named Val. In the scene, Hillary-as-Val gets to poke fun at her public image as impersonal and out of touch with lines to Kate such as, "You give off such a young, cool vibe, you must work in Brooklyn." And Kate-as-Hillary gets to deliver keenly understated, but constructive, criticism of the real candidate:

VAL: *It really is great how long you've supported gay marriage.*

HILLARY: *I could have supported it sooner.*

VAL: *Well, you did pretty soon.*

HILLARY: *Could'a been sooner.*

VAL: *Fair point.*

Kate has more than celebrity and political impersonations in her back pocket on *SNL*. She grew a crop of delightfully weird characters, such as the shaggy-haired, middle-aged woman Colleen Rafferty—the only person in a group of alien abductees whose alien encounters are darkly and perversely hilarious. Another is the Russian woman, Olya Povlatsky, who visits the Weekend Update news desk to comment on happenings that are relatively mundane, compared to the catastrophe and hardship she has faced living in her small, Russian village. In a segment about the 2014 Sochi Olympics, Olya remarks that she had been to Sochi one time, "to throw myself into the sea, but the line was too long." This panopoly of nuanced characters—ones that are simultaneously silly, thoughtful, smart, and complicated—ultimately earned her two Emmy Awards for Outstanding Supporting Actress in a Comedy Series.

The chance for Kate to flex her physical comedy chops on the big screen came in 2016 when she played the brilliantly bizarre engineer character Jillian Holtzmann in Paul Feig's *Ghostbusters*. Stealing scenes left and right with little more than the pop of her eyes or a quick lick of her proton-ghost-zapping gun, Kate's Holtzmann exudes complete confidence and pride in her quirkiness. She's an awesome freak and her power lies in the fact that she knows it and she's not afraid to show it. Her joyful, comic swagger makes Holtzmann and, by extension, Kate McKinnon, the kind of masterful funny woman whose most inspiring and empowering character might just be herself.

"I was just never discouraged from doing something wacky like trying to be a comedian."

— KATE MCKINNON

LUCILLE BALL

[AUGUST 6, 1911–APRIL 26, 1989]

At first it seems like a snap: the chocolates come out on a conveyor belt and each one gets wrapped in a piece of wax paper, continuing out of sight into another room. "This is easy!" says Lucy Ricardo to her best friend, Ethel Mertz. The two have made a bet with their husbands—Ricky and Fred, respectively—that they would have an easier time earning a paycheck out in the "real world" than the boys would managing everyday household duties.

A supervisor has warned Lucy and Ethel that if one chocolate makes it through to the next room unwrapped, the two women would be fired. Lucy and Ethel successfully wrap chocolates for about sixty seconds before the belt starts to speed up slightly. In an instant, both women are grabbing chocolates off the belt, shoving them into their blouses, and cramming them into their mouths; Lucy even takes off her pillowy chef's hat as part of her uniform and jams candies inside. The belt stops. *Relief.* The supervisor comes in to check on the women and, pleased to see the results, congratulates them before hollering, "Speed it up!" Lucy's eyes bulge in mock fright. Chocolates begin hurtling along the conveyer belt at an alarming rate. Faces filled with bonbons, Lucy and Ethel resume franti-

cally shoving chocolate in every place chocolate can fit. Meanwhile, the studio audience is squealing with laughter. This *I Love Lucy* episode, "Switching Jobs," became one of Lucille Ball's most famous pieces of comedy, but hardly her most outrageous.

As a young girl growing up in Celoron, New York, Lucille Ball was no stranger to the world of entertainment. She often went to see the traveling vaudeville shows, full of acrobats, song-and-dance teams, and comedians who came to Celoron Park—a popular amusement and theater pavilion just outside of town. At the age of twelve, Lucy got her first chance to take the stage and was hooked. By the age of fifteen she was enrolled in the John Murray Anderson School for the Dramatic Arts in New York City. Surely she was on her way to becoming a big-time star!

Spoiler alert: She was not on her way to becoming a big-time star quite yet.

Drama school was a disaster for Lucy. She was anxious and often tongue-tied around her teachers and her peers—this might have had something to do with taking classes alongside another young actress already earning a fair amount of recognition named Bette Davis. The instructors were tough, but not like a grumpy-but-lovable-mentor kind of tough, more like Simon Cowell–on–season–1–of–*American Idol*–makes–you–cry kind of tough. Labeling her skills and talent weak at best, they felt Lucy did not have what it took to be a serious actress. She cut her losses in New York, died her brown hair blonde, and headed out West to try her luck in America's dream factory: Hollywood.

Lucy found Hollywood marginally more welcoming than New York. She worked in movies on a variety of forgettable pictures wacky wife Liz Cugat. Every week, listeners tuned in to find out what crazy scheme Liz had cooked up and what hilarious way she came up with to resolve the caper. As Lucy delivered arch quips, witty one-liners, and silly voices in funny accents, from inside the recording studio she could see the producers and sound guys shaking with laughter. Maybe those drama teachers were right, and the type of "serious" Lucille Ball was meant for involved serious laughter.

"*I'm not funny, I'm brave.*"
—LUCILLE BALL

in mostly small or supporting roles. At one point, the studio encouraged her to dye her hair red to help her stand out a bit more. She even met and fell in love with a fella—a dashing Cuban bandleader named Desi Arnaz, who shared her passion and drive to be in show business. Still, Lucy longed for a larger career, a chance to shine the way she knew she could. Unbeknownst to the redhead, that career was just ahead through the next set of lights.

The year was 1948. Lucy had landed a role on a popular weekly radio serial, called *My Favorite Husband*, playing the part of the *My Favorite Husband* was an enormous success. It caught the attention of producers from CBS who invited Lucy to develop the show for television, an exciting new medium at the time. Lucy agreed on one condition: that her then-husband, Desi Arnaz, would play the role of her television husband, Ricky Ricardo. The network balked. They wanted Lucy, but were not sold on having Ricky along for the ride. Lucy and Desi responded with a polite but firm, "It's both of us or neither of us." When the network wouldn't budge, the two took their material and natural chemistry and worked out a version of the show for live audiences at vaudeville theaters. The show was a hit with the theater crowd, a minor detail that CBS could not ignore. They approached the couple again, admitting that maybe they had made just the tiniest "oopsie." On October 15, 1951, *I Love Lucy* made its way into America's living rooms and sitcom television would never be the same.

I Love Lucy was a renegade show on so many levels: Lucy and Desi insisted on shooting the show in Hollywood, rather than New York, where most shows were produced. When the studio pushed back over the expense, the couple took a pay cut to cover the costs. They also used a live studio audience, instead of a laugh track of prerecorded audience laughter. The live element of working with an audience amplified the energy of Lucy's comic antics that were almost always physically rigorous and outrageous. *I Love Lucy* was also the first sitcom to use a three-camera approach to shooting the show, which allowed the directors to film scenes in sequence.

Of course, the biggest rebel of the show was Lucy herself, who beguiled and surprised audiences as the not-your-average housewife Lucy Ricardo. As the zealous, ambitious, hilariously stubborn Lucy Ricardo, Lucille

Ball literally stretched her comedy muscles with physical humor unlike anything done by women onscreen since the slapstick actresses of early silent films. Lucy stomping grapes in a giant vat and getting into a messy, pulverized grape wrestling match with the other woman in the tub; turning herself into a human popsicle after getting locked in a meat freezer; staring cross-eyed down a fake rubber nose as it catches on fire from a lit cigarette; trying to walk down an enormous spiral staircase while wearing a ten-pound showgirl headdress. When it came to laughs, Lucy had no limits.

This also applied to the way Lucy felt about handling certain social conventions on television, namely pregnancy. For network executives, the depiction of a pregnant woman on television was a taboo right up there with flag burning and satanic ritual. Lucy would have none of this nonsense. Rather than have her written out of the show in some lame story line about going to visit her mother for three months, she insisted on taking her full-frontal pregnancy into living rooms across America. The network did not like the term "pregnant," labeling it much too vulgar for audiences (just wait a couple of decades, 1950s TV executives, you ain't seen nothing yet); instead, they had the writers use "expecting." Thus Lucy became one of the first women in a major sitcom "expecting" on national television.

I Love Lucy ran for six seasons, from 1951 to 1957, and won five Emmy awards. After the show ended, Lucy continued to be a fixture in television programs and feature films, including two with Desi. She lived out the rest of her life revered and respected as one of comedy's "first ladies" for the ground she broke as both a leader in the entertainment industry and as a funny woman. In her role as Lucy Ricardo, Lucille Ball invited women to laugh at, but more importantly, laugh *with* Lucy. Her wacky, messy antics were ways of slyly breaking down ideas of domestic perfection and, at the same time, undermining notions of the ideal wife, mother, and woman that would alter the lives of generations forever.

GILDA RADNER

[JUNE 28, 1946–MAY 20, 1989]

The lovable characters came spilling out of Gilda Radner like clowns tumbling out of a circus car—Roseanne Roseannadanna, Emily Litella, Lisa Loopner, and Candy Slice. Her creations were as silly, darling, and vulnerable as Gilda herself, who lived to laugh and made it her life's purpose to bring the power of that joy to the masses. And when her worst fears came true, receiving a diagnosis of ovarian cancer in 1986, Gilda wrote a best-selling book about her illness, titled *It's Always Something*, to keep the world laughing along with her through the pain.

Gilda dropped out of the University of Michigan in her senior year to move to Toronto, and get involved in the growing local theater scene. She won a role in the ensemble musical *Godspell*, a rock musical based on the Christian gospels according to Saint Matthew (it's the Bible with guitar solos). In *Godspell*, Gilda was surrounded by relatively unknown performers, including Eugene Levy, Andrea Martin, and Martin Short, who later became comic stand-outs in the Canadian sketch show *Second City TV (SCTV)*. Through her new friends, Gilda found out about Second City's training center in Toronto. She enrolled in classes, learning the finer points of the kind of playful comedy that came to her so naturally.

Gilda's circle of funny friends expanded quickly to include Dan Ackroyd, Harold Ramis, and John Belushi, all of whom were young unknowns with a hunger for making people laugh. She followed this herd of comedians to New York City, all hoping to break into the comedy scene there. Once in the city, Gilda got involved in something called *The National Lampoon Radio Hour*.

While the world waited around for podcasts to get invented, they fused their ears to the radio, tuning in to radio serials. *The National Lampoon Radio Hour* was a weekly show based on Harvard University's comedy magazine of the same name. The *Lampoon Radio Hour* was filled with gross-out, juvenile, sometimes bad—in the sense of both taste and political correctness—comedy. The program led to a live touring sketch comedy show, *The National Lampoon Show*. With a lot of the same humor and jokes recycled for live performance, the show was not going to earn anyone awards or even favorable reviews, but it was one of the first times Gilda debuted her Barbara Walters impersonation and, more importantly, it brought her to the attention of a young Canadian guy looking to cast funny people for a new network television show. That guy was Lorne Michaels. The show would eventually be *Saturday Night Live* and Gilda would be one of its original cast members.

It's hard to imagine a television world without *Saturday Night Live,* but until 1975 that was the reality, which is why, when it debuted in the fall, people thought Michaels's show was as different and memorable as tabasco-flavored ice cream. The rumor was that the show was being called "edgy" because of these long-haired young people making jokes about drug culture, politics, and anything considered "lame" by the standards of young people (which is nearly everything). Ready for whatever this thing was that Michaels had helped cook up in a comedy lab, Gilda joined Laraine Newman, Jane Curtin, John Belushi, Chevy Chase, Dan Ackroyd, and Garrett Morris to bring viewers a new kind of sketch comedy that was irreverent, risky, and socially as well as politically hip.

For Gilda, *SNL* was her personal comedy playground. Over the course of her five years on the show, she danced, sang, giggled, and somersaulted into America's hearts and living rooms each week. Gilda brought us one of the most memorable, awkwardly geeky teen girls with Lisa Loopner. Played opposite her "friend," Todd DiLaMuca (Bill Murray), Lisa forever endured noogies while trading lame jokes and puns with the equally awkward and obnoxious Todd.

She unleashed the brassy commentator Roseanne Roseannadanna at the Weekend Update desk, helmed by Dan Ackroyd and Jane Curtin. Outfitted with an enormous wig of frizzy black hair and a smart, gray suit, Gilda's Roseanne Roseannadanna answered viewer mail about topics of current interest. In reality, it was the same viewer's name she read each time: Richard Feder from New Jersey (which was an in joke; that was the name of writer Alan Zweibel's brother-in-law). As she ruthlessly chomped on her gum, Roseanne's response quickly digressed into lengthy, meandering anecdotes that gave her an excuse to talk about something inappropriate and disgusting, like getting food stuck in your teeth. As Curtin tried to reel her back in to her original point, Roseanne would cheerfully shrug and respond, "Well, it just goes to show you, it's always something." Roseanne was cheeky and unapologetic; she said the awkward thing that everyone else was already thinking, which made her both brave and admirable.

And then there was the spritelike little girl, Judy Miller, who put on elaborate shows and scenarios in the confines of her bedroom. The Judy Miller character distilled the beautiful anarchy of Gilda's improvisation training in the way that Gilda-as-Judy wholly embraced whatever in the scene caught her attention. In some ways, audiences were witnessing Gilda at her essence: a playful girl happily bounding from fantasy to fantasy, riding an unending wave of pure imagination and silliness.

When she left *SNL*, Gilda took many of her characters with her to perform them in her one-woman show, *Gilda Radner—Live from New York*. The show became a film titled *Gilda Live!* directed by Mike Nichols and released in theaters in 1980. While the film was viewed as a box-office bust, it gave audiences the chance to enjoy Gilda's singular sweetness as the kind of funny woman whose performances were simply joyful.

As Gilda faced the terror of her cancer diagnosis, she armed herself with laughter as a shield against despair and hopelessness. As part of her treatment, she became involved in a wellness community, a support group for patients and survivors. She fed them jokes. She found she could slip easily into Roseanne

> *"Life is about not knowing, having to change, taking the moment and making the best of it, without knowing what's going to happen next."*
>
> —GILDA RADNER

Roseannadanna to make the group laugh, and wasn't this the epitome of "It's always something," anyway?

Out of Gilda's tragic passing, Gilda's Club—an organization of local support groups for cancer patients and their families—was established in 1995. And out of Gilda's career in comedy came generations of women who cite her as their influence, their hero, their first comedy crushes, and, in so many cases, the reason they decided to follow her example and stitch together a life and career devoted to laughter.

DAUNTLESS, DEFIANT, DARINGLY DISRUPTIVE

SARAH SILVERMAN

CHELSEA HANDLER

AMY SCHUMER

MAE WEST

KATHY GRIFFIN

MOMS MABLEY

MARGARET CHO

ALI WONG

JOAN RIVERS

ILANA GLAZER AND ABBI JACOBSON

SANDRA BERNHARD

Comedy rebels, joke renegades, humor hellions—these are the funny women who never met a line they didn't mind obliterating. Controversy? That's a breakfast snack for this set. Going too far? Never heard of it. Cringe-worthy. Pure flattery. The disruptors of comedy go all-in to talk about the dark, difficult, and taboo topics that make us anxious, like racism, religion, violence, and sexual assault. They also bring their own brave to the stage or page in their willingness to put their personal experiences with challenging, tragic, or disturbing issues in the spotlight. In short: These women *go there* with equal parts ferocity and fearlessness. Inviting people to laugh at pain or hard truths is a risk for both the comic and the audience. Remember, these women are extraordinary, but they're not invincible; in many cases it's their hearts and egos that are in play as they dare to speak truth to power and open up spaces for difficult conversations.

But it's more than just material for these envelope-pushing comics. Many of these women challenge the status quo in the comedy industry by going against cultural and gender stereotypes. They break ground by doing comedy in innovative ways—adding in songs or monologues; performing while seven months' pregnant; using a DIY grassroots approach to putting a sitcom online. And they openly defy or unsettle the entrenched systems of power, designed to suppress and mitigate women's voices, experiences, and contributions. Who knew comedy could do all that? These women do and they aren't about to let us forget it anytime soon.

EXTRA EXTRAORDINAIRES: Lea DeLaria · Hannah Gadsby · Whitney Cummings · Janeane Garofalo · Michelle Wolf · Jenny Yang · Lisa Lampanelli · Mo'Nique · Carrie Fisher · Tiffany Haddish · Alexis Wilkinson · Rebel Wilson · Megan Mullally · Patti Harrison

SARAH SILVERMAN

[DECEMBER 1, 1970–]

Sarah Silverman was fired. Wait, it gets worse: She was fired from her dream job. Wait, it gets even worse: She was fired from her dream job via *fax*, which is basically an ancient way of sending texts by paper. The worst. Sarah was only twenty-two years old when she was plucked out of the stand-up scene and hired as a writer/performer for *Saturday Night Live*. It was a gig that she had wanted since she was a teenager growing up in New Hampshire watching Gilda Radner, Jane Curtin, Dan Ackroyd, and the rest of the legendary comedians on TV in her parents' living room. Sarah was ready to take her place in the history of "Not Ready for Prime Time Players," except for one small wrinkle: *SNL* wasn't ready for her.

Struggling to get her writing to air and only appearing as a performer in a handful of sketches, Sarah was let go after one season. No matter how it shakes out, getting dumped chafes. Sarah took all she learned from that experience and got back to the business of making people laugh her way: by creating edgy, provocative comedy, forged from some of the culture's most taboo social and political topics.

Sarah performed her first stand-up set at a club in Boston when she was barely out of high school. After graduation, she enrolled in New York University to study drama, but found her real education in the nightclubs and grimy basement stages of open-mic comedy clubs in the city. She dropped out of college and put all her energy into a comedy career, which began to pay off when she got the call from *SNL*. Though her tenure on the show was short-lived, it was where she got to meet and work with a lot of other funny people, including a writer who shared Sarah's sharp, twisted sense of humor: Bob Odenkirk (*Breaking Bad* and *Better Call Saul*).

After parting ways with *SNL,* Sarah doubled down on her stand-up. She also took a job working on HBO's sketch comedy *Mr. Show with Bob and David*, written, starring, and created by Odenkirk and fellow comic and writer David Cross. The show featured nervy, irreverently funny sketches that satirized subjects like religion, relationships, and family values. Everything done on *Mr. Show* had a twisted angle to it, turning benign scenarios, such as a job interview or a first date, into something weirdly unexpected. It's hardly a shocker that *Mr. Show* was an ideal place for Sarah to lend her creative voice and further develop her distinctive comic style.

When she wasn't working on TV, Sarah

was burning up comedy stages across the country. She had quickly earned a reputation as a funny woman with a strong and often controversial point of view to her material. Jokes about the Holocaust or sexual assault came delivered through Sarah's cheerful, plucky performance persona, designed to disarm audiences and make them receptive to considering the bigger issues and questions raised by her incendiary comedy. In this respect, Sarah was a little like Mary Poppins singing about how a spoonful of sugar makes the medicine go down, only in this case it was truth wrapped in laughter and, also, with a lot more swearing and vagina jokes.

This was on full display in Sarah's 2005 stand-up film special, *Jesus Is Magic*. On the show, Sarah audaciously upends everything from AIDS and sex to the tragedy of 9/11, presented with her signature beguiling demeanor as if she were just the girl next door, curled up on the couch with a cup of tea, talking casually about society's most terrible and disturbing happenings.

Critics were divided on *Jesus Is Magic*. Some felt Sarah's shocking material was a gimmick. Others found her comedy incredibly smart. Her material was vulgar, but it had substance; her jokes encouraged people to question and challenge the status quo. Everyone agreed on one thing: Sarah belonged among the ranks of comics like Kathy Griffin, Joan Rivers, and Margaret Cho, outspoken funny women who thrived on comedy that was blunt, honest, and uncomfortable. If anything, Sarah's detractors—whether they were media critics, other comedians, or audience members—fueled her drive to continue breaking the rules of comedy, which is what she did with her scripted show for Comedy Central, *The Sarah Silverman Program*.

The Sarah Silverman Program transported Sarah's onstage stand-up persona—one she has described in interviews as someone who is very ignorant and very arrogant—to the small screen. Playing a kicky, freeloading, irresponsible woman named Sarah, stumbling through life with a group of quirky friends, the show essentially brought viewers into Sarah's sunny, bent mind and offensive, overly simplified worldview. Sarah's character was immature, crass, and hilariously truthful in her blissful cluelessness, which became a clever way of critiquing stereotypes and prejudices. The show ran for three seasons and brought Sarah an Emmy nomination. It also put Sarah in a position of creative power within the industry: She helmed an unconventional sitcom designed around humor and topics specifically meant to unsettle everything people knew about comedy made by a woman.

Sarah continues to rack up acclaim and expand her material. Her 2013 HBO stand-up special, *We Are Miracles*, won an Emmy for Outstanding Writing for a Variety Special and her dramatic role in the film *I Smile Back* got Sarah a Screen Actors Guild Award

a series in 2017 titled *I Love You, America*. The show has a late-night-TV type of format with interviews, monologues, guests, and filmed segments that include people from all walks of life with many different political and cultural perspectives. For Sarah, visiting with a conservative, Trump-supporting family from Louisiana is not about exploiting people in the name of picking low-hanging joke fruit; it's about Sarah finally realizing the true

"I don't set out to offend or shock, but I also don't do anything to avoid it."
— SARAH SILVERMAN

nomination. As she's developed as a comedian, Sarah has tempered *some* of her swagger with a bit more vulnerability. In her best-selling memoir *The Bedwetter: Stories of Courage, Redemption, and Pee,* Sarah candidly and humorously discusses her struggles growing up as a chronic bed-wetter and her battles with depression and mental illness.

Sarah has also thrown her biting humor behind work as a political activist. The 2016 US election left Americans dealing with deep rifts. Never one to back away from contentious ground, Sarah loped into the fray with

power of her gifts and skills: using humor as the lever to open up a space of compassion and, possibly, meaningful change.

Sarah serves up her definitely "not ready for prime time" material to give people permission to find humor in the differences that we use to drive wedges between one another. Her dark comedy makes us laugh, but it also makes us think, question, and challenge the big concepts, like racism and religious expression. No wonder Sarah and her big, bold, brash comedy couldn't quite fit on the little old soundstage of Studio 8-H.

CHELSEA HANDLER

[FEBRUARY 25, 1975–]

A lot of comedians take a pause from performing stand-up regularly or working on a TV show to take on other comedy-related projects. They write a book, star in a film, or produce someone else's work. Few include "political activism" on that list. But, then again, few are like the audacious Chelsea Handler. Chelsea has always been a fiercely outspoken advocate for the LGBTQ community. In the months following the 2016 US presidential election, which to many people came across as a serious record scratch across much of the progress made by civil rights policies, Chelsea knew she needed to take action. In the fall of 2017, Chelsea wrapped her successful Netflix talk show, *Chelsea,* and got involved in the political scene, lending her voice to statewide races to help get more women elected to office. Known for her caustic, sarcastic, excoriating style of comedy, aimed at taking down celebrities and other entertainment figures, Chelsea was going to put the full force of her acerbic wit in play on the campaign trail. A "Handler 2020" run for office wouldn't even be the weirdest or worst thing to make headlines.

Long before she was hustling for democracy, Chelsea was trying to break into the LA show business scene. She had come to California by way of New Jersey, a recent high school graduate set on pursuing an acting career in Hollywood. While waitressing to support herself, Chelsea unsuccessfully chased audition after audition in hopes of getting her foot in the door. Strangely enough, it took a run-in with the law to open up Chelsea's perspective about using her natural, darkly tinged sense of humor for a career. Arrested for driving under the influence, Chelsea was mandated to attend a class about the dangers of drinking and driving. When she relayed her, let's face it, humiliating and very serious story to her fellow classmates, she did so the only way she knew how—with self-deprecating, honest humor. Chelsea's capacity to acknowledge her mistake in a way that broke the tension resonated with people in the class. They laughed and Chelsea took note. Maybe comedy was where she belonged.

Chelsea began making the rounds at area comedy clubs, winning over audiences with her blunt, biting brand of stand-up. Steady bookings gave way to TV roles, including a part on an all-female reality show for the Oxygen network, titled *Girls Behaving Badly.* In it, the cast played silly pranks on unsuspecting people. Though she was part of an ensemble cast, Chelsea's cutting humor and outspoken nature made her stand out. She became a singular kind of presence on the comedy club circuit as well as on her appearances on *The Tonight Show with Jay Leno* and other late-night stages.

While Chelsea continued to build her career working in TV, film, and onstage, she also poured her comic voice onto the page. Her first essay collection, *My Horizontal Life: A Collection of One-Night Stands* (2005), quickly became a *New York Times* best seller.

a handful of women to have their own late-night comedy shows. For seven seasons, Chelsea, along with a revolving group of funny panelists, dissected pop culture happenings as if they were presiding over a roast, leaving no celebrity or hot trend unscathed amid their scorching, comic commentary. The show also featured an interview segment between Chelsea and a special guest who was rarely any match for her quick, provocative banter. *Chelsea Lately* gave Chelsea free rein as a cre-

"I'm very much about letting other people shine, because it makes us all shine brighter."

—CHELSEA HANDLER

She went on to write four other books, including *Are You There, Vodka? It's Me, Chelsea* (2009) and *Chelsea Chelsea Bang Bang* (2011). Chelsea humorously excoriates herself in the same way she lambastes many of her comic subjects in these books that are part memoir and part funny, unfiltered commentary on the social and cultural trends that affect us all.

Chelsea made comedy history in 2007 when she launched her own late-night show, *Chelsea Lately* on E!, joining the ranks of only

ative and a comedian. It highlighted her gift for shaking things up and showing the power and influence funny women wield.

Chelsea's voice and her no-holds-barred approach to comedy put her in the lineage of funny women like Joan Rivers and Whoopi Goldberg, who disrupted the idea that women are supposed to be chaste, passive, or quiet. Chelsea said, "Thanks, but no thanks" to those attitudes with every searing zinger, every off-color joke, and every unsavory arch remark she leveled at her audiences.

AMY SCHUMER

[JUNE 1, 1981–]

They're called "roasts" for a reason. Your closest friends gather together in your honor and pile on nasty, vulgar, tasteless comedic insults, like feeding logs to a bonfire with you tied to a stake in the middle of the flames. This is their way of showing how much they love and respect you. Brutal. Roasts not only embody a hipness factor, but a lot of people actually consider them one of the best ways to pay tribute to someone. These are possibly the same people who

their time in the hot seat with the same relish they enjoy cuing up zingers to celebrate the roastee. Amy Schumer is one of those women. In 2003, Comedy Central revived the televised roast phenomenon, and in 2011 Amy outshone many of the male comics in the room gathered for Charlie Sheen's roast, with her dark and lethally honest brand of comedy.

Amy's roast appearance for Charlie Sheen wasn't her first TV appearance. She had been working as a stand-up comedian in New York

> "I say if I'm beautiful. I say if I'm strong. You will not determine my story—I will."
>
> —AMY SCHUMER

also think giving someone a Groupon for bowling lessons is one of the best ways to say "I love you."

Comedy roasts of famous funny people and celebrities became popular in the 1970s when NBC aired several Dean Martin Celebrity Roast specials. The legendary entertainer gathered a group of celebrity friends to roast a fellow superstar, like Frank Sinatra, Jackie Gleason, and even Ronald Reagan. Though roasts can be seen as testosterone-fueled events, there are plenty of women who enjoy

for several years before appearing on the reality show competition, *Last Comic Standing,* in 2007, where she came in a very respectable fourth place and earned a ton of recognition. Her stand-up career picked up steam and in 2011 the producers at Comedy Central offered her the gig as one of the roasters. The way she gamely leveled Sheen during the roast, pulling no punches in her bawdy jokes about the actor's infamous antics and ongoing scandals proved that she didn't just push the envelope with her comedy, she incinerated it.

Amy's brash, uninhibited comedic voice found a permanent home on TV with the launch of her own show for Comedy Central in 2013, *Inside Amy Schumer*. The show featured sketches, stand-up, and person-on-the-street-type interviews. The show ran for three years and gifted viewers with some incredibly smart, savvy, provocative comedy about topics as controversial as Bill Cosby's sexual assault allegations and rape culture in general.

Onstage as well as in interviews, Amy has talked openly about being drawn to subjects that people avoid talking about, especially sex. She is one of a growing number of women comedians interested in using humor to have frank, open conversations about sexuality in general and about women's sexual experiences in particular. For Amy, it's not about doing material that's "shocking" in a purely sensational way; it's about mining for deeper truths and shattering preconceived notions about both femininity and funny women.

Inside Amy Schumer also elegantly blended feminist politics and viewpoints with an off-color comedic slant on issues surrounding body image, misogyny, hookup practices, religion, and the relentless and ridiculous double standard foisted upon women across the entertainment industry. The show allowed Amy to continue to refine her comedic voice, but it also showcased her talents as a comedic actress.

Amy's comedic acting chops came out in full force in the 2015 film *Trainwreck*. Amy wrote and starred in the romcom about a writer and perennial party girl, played by Amy, who has spent most of her life dodging commitment and romantic responsibility. This all changes when she meets a prestigious sports doctor played by Bill Hader. Despite its typical romcom premise, *Trainwreck* gave audiences a very atypical female lead in Amy, who brought all her black wit and raw authenticity to depict a flawed, funny, complicated woman whom female viewers related to.

Amy brought more of the same to the 2017 flick, *Snatched*, starring alongside comic icon Goldie Hawn. In the film, Amy and Goldie play a mother-daughter duo who get caught up in an inane series of dangerous escapades while on a vacation in Ecuador. *Snatched* put Amy's guerrilla style of comedy front and center in a film that also showcased two strong, funny female leads driving the kind of action, plot, and outrageous antics often reserved for male "buddy" films.

An outspoken critic of the ludicrous body

image ideals imposed on women, Amy has deployed her caustic humor to take on detractors who have disparaged her for not meeting unattainable physical and beauty standards. Her acceptance speech for the 2015 *Glamour* magazine Woman of the Year Award included some hilarious, profanity-laced comments about the media's role (including that of women's magazines) in stoking women's negative, toxic self-perceptions.

Her 2018 film *I Feel Pretty* explored this notion a bit further. Amy plays an insecure woman named Renee longing to be one of the rarified, "perfect" beautiful women plastered on the covers of magazines. One day Renee suffers a head injury in an exercise class and when she regains consciousness, she looks at her reflection to see someone in the mirror who is drop-dead gorgeous. However, to everyone else she looks exactly the same. Renee's newfound confidence gives her the uninhibited courage to go after everything she wants—the perfect job, the perfect guy, the cool group of friends—until, of course, she discovers that perfection is a myth. It's a movie that aims to hammer home the message of loving the skin you're in, one that Amy feels particularly strongly about as a woman who has dealt with her share of body image criticism.

For the woman who had built a career on shining a light into the dark corners, it made complete sense for Amy to turn that introspection on herself. Her memoir, *The Girl with the Lower Back Tattoo*, was published in 2016 and quickly became a *New York Times* best seller. Mixing memoir with personal advice, Amy covers a wide range of personal and professional experiences, from dealing with serious illness in her family to her fraught relationship with her mother. She also shares her thoughts on cultural issues, such as gun and domestic violence, demonstrating that humor can do more than make people laugh— it can make people think, care, and maybe even take action.

Whether writing books, screenplays, sketches, or new stand-up material, or simply being in her element onstage, Amy shows up as her most authentic self, allowing people to share in the challenges and profound joys that come with being a professional funny woman.

MAE WEST

[AUGUST 17, 1893–NOVEMBER 22, 1980]

The title of the play: *Sex*. The lead character: a prostitute. The year: 1926. What could possibly go wrong? Mae West was only too happy to find out. She was the writer, director, producer, and had the starring role of prostitute in this controversial new play to hit New York's Broadway. When it came to breaking all the rules, no one did it with such style, flair, and obvious relish as Mae. This play was no exception. People became unhinged at the idea that Mae, in all her sassy, voluptuous, comically licentious glory, would perform a character in a play about the sinful, morally bankrupt, not to mention highly illegal, life and exploits of a prostitute. The complaints from religious groups escalated into a howl, prompting city officials to raid the theater, shut down the show, and haul Mae off to jail on "morals charges." It was a travesty! It was scandalous! It was the kind of publicity that Mae could only dream of getting.

Instead of paying a small fine, Mae opted to spend ten days in jail. She milked her time behind bars for all it was worth to the press. She granted interviews to reporters, telling them she dined with the warden and his wife and, because she was something of a star, was allowed to wear silk underwear instead of the standard-issue prison burlap. Mae made it out of the clink after eight days for "good behavior," which is about as ironic as it gets for America's first bad girl of comedy.

By age fourteen, Mae had already shown herself to be a skilled singer, dancer, and comic actress on vaudeville stages. She made her Broadway debut in 1911, singing and dancing in the revues *A la Broadway* and *Hello, Paris*. Though the shows closed after eight performances, a reviewer for the *New York Times* singled out Mae as an engaging and talented dancer/actress. The press helped Mae land several other roles, including a breakout part in a very popular revue, titled *Sometime*, where she starred opposite Ed Wynn, one of the leading comics of the day. *Sometime* featured Mae's character performing an incredibly daring, extremely alluring dance called "the shimmy." It was exactly what you think: shaking your shoulders in time to the music. Shocking. Very NC-17. But in 1918 it was titillating and unnerving to watch a woman having great fun and taking great pleasure in moving her body in such a suggestive way. Mae's performance was so popular that when they printed the sheet music to sell in stores to the public, they put her image on the front of the song, "Ev'rybody Shimmies Now," from the play. Mae had found her naughty niche.

She began writing her own plays, such as the infamous *Sex* and then later *The Drag*, a "comedy drama" that dealt with homosexual themes. Mae was an early and longtime supporter of women's and gay rights. To no one's surprise, *The Drag* was banned in New York, thanks in part to the New York Society for the Suppression of Vice. Suppressing anything resembling pleasure, especially physical pleasure, was a very big pastime for social,

who expertly combined wit and an admirable kind of swagger with raw, sexual energy considered forbidden for most women. There was only one place big enough for Mae's supernova persona: the silver screen.

Mae was already forty (which is about seventy million in Hollywood actress years) when she landed her first starring role. Rather than try to compete with the young, lithe ingenues surging into film studios, Mae flaunted her

> *"You only live once, but if you do it right, once is enough."*
>
> — MAE WEST

religious, and civic groups in the early 1900s. But all would find out soon enough that no one could suppress Mae West.

Throughout the 1920s and early 1930s, Mae continued writing plays, including *The Wicked Age*, *The Pleasure Man*, and *The Constant Sinner* (three guesses what these were all about). Ultimately, Mae was destined for more success on the stage and screen than as a writer. Her role as the smart, racy, sexually empowered character Diamond Lil in a play by the same name became a Broadway sensation. It solidified Mae's image as an actress

curvaceous, hourglass figure and embraced the strong, funny, suggestive performance style she had honed in her stage roles. Her characters were early representations of the kind of sexually potent, socially and economically empowered, independent women who would show up in films in the twenty-first century as bosses, badasses, and total ass-kickers. The women Mae portrayed dwarfed their male and female costars. Predictably, she stole every scene, if not the entire movie itself, with little more than a snappy one-liner or the slow saunter of her hips as she made her exit.

Among some of Mae's best and most hilariously arch dialogue from her movies were some that she wrote herself:

From *Night after Night* (1932)

HAT-CHECK GIRL: *Goodness! What beautiful diamonds!*

MAE (AS MAUDIE TRIPLETT): *Goodness had nothing to do with it, dearie.*

From *She Done Him Wrong* (1933)

CAPTAIN CUMMINGS: *Haven't you ever met a man who could make you happy?*

MAE (AS LADY LOU): *Sure, lots of times.*

And from the same flick, Mae delivered a line that would live in infamy:

LADY LOU: *Is that a pistol in your pocket or are you just happy to see me?*

Mae worked steadily in film throughout the 1930s and '40s, despite encountering criticism and even threats of legal action for the kinds of female characters she portrayed. She also drew fire for the subject matter of her films, which often featured dicey material about sex, unwed mothers, and religion—sometimes all in the same movie!

By 1934 the movie industry had imple-mented something called the Production Code: a stringent set of standardized moral and ethical guidelines for all films. Essentially, a complete and total buzzkill. Screenplays, especially those dealing with controversial topics, themes, or depictions, were heavily censored or rejected entirely. For instance, Mae's 1934 film *It Ain't No Sin* had its title changed to the more palatable *Belle of the Nineties*. Lame. Mae knew it was so much weak sauce and went against everything she stood for as a proud, independent woman. So she began to purposely "troll" censors by overloading her screenplays with insanely suggestive dialogue. She knew they would end up carving the scripts to bits, but was determined to have a few laughs at their uptight expenses along the way.

The relentless censorship led to many battles between Mae and studio heads who were too afraid to produce and back her films. Weak sauce extreme. The constant tension and never-ending conflicts eventually took their toll on Mae. She left film and went back to performing on the live stage while also doing radio work.

But Mae's ribald humor had become something like a third ear—it was an insepara-ble part of her and her uncompromising creativity. Radio was no less censorship-friendly than film. In one radio sketch, Mae played opposite the ventriloquist Edgar Bergen and his wooden "dummy," Charlie McCarthy. In the exchange between the two, Mae quips that she found Charlie "all wood and a yard long." She goes on to coyly remark: "Charles, I remember our last date, and I have the splinters to prove it!" Damn, Mae West! You went there! This type of risqué material from Mae did nothing to endear her to moral and religious groups as well as critics, censors, and radio executives worried about finding themselves out of work.

Despite the "trouble" Mae caused throughout the entertainment industry, she worked into the final years of her life. She moved in and out of film, television, and stage shows. She even recorded two music albums in the early-1970s and published her memoir, *Goodness Has Nothing to Do with It.*

Mae remains a celebrated and revered woman for the way she changed and challenged film and comedy, ridiculing sexual and social mores from the point of view of a fearless, modern, self-assured woman who spoke volumes with little more than the curve of her smile and the shake of her supple shoulders.

KATHY GRIFFIN

[NOVEMBER 4, 1960–]

When Kathy Griffin was eighteen, she persuaded her parents to move from Illinois to California so she could pursue an acting career. These are not the actions of a shrinking violet. But it wouldn't be Kathy's boldest or most radical act. In fact, Kathy's career in comedy would become a lifelong chronicle of what happens when women insist on telling their truths about the world from their own singular, and, in the case of Kathy, sometimes unpopular or even shocking perspectives.

Kathy's experiences performing in high school musical theater productions sparked her interest in acting. The family's move to Los Angeles put Kathy at ground zero for film and television. It also introduced her to the renowned improvisational comedy troupe and improv theater, called the Groundlings. Kathy attended a show and was immediately entranced by the group of funny people onstage; this was her tribe. She enrolled in classes while simultaneously developing material for stand-up. Throughout the late 1980s and the early 1990s, Kathy performed regularly at LA comedy clubs and even ran one of her own stand-up showcases, titled "Hot Cup of Talk," along with another emerging stand-up named Janeane Garofalo.

Kathy continued to build her career in TV and onstage doing stand-up. She landed a role as the snarky, savage restaurant critic on the NBC sitcom *Suddenly Susan* and made several appearances in a minor role on *The Fresh Prince of Bel-Air*. But it was onstage where Kathy most aggressively evolved her signature comedic style and novel comic voice. She was unapologetically brash in her act, no matter what the topic, but when she began to add more material about her funny, sometimes embarrassing, personal experiences as a "D-list" level celebrity, she found her comedy really start to take off.

No one was off-limits for Kathy. She gleefully embellished gossipy anecdotes and let fly scorching takedowns of all types of celebrities and public figures, no matter where they sat on Hollywood's alphabet hierarchy (A-list, D-list, or Z-list), like the original Queen of Pop, Madonna:

Have you guys noticed Madonna is British now? She was doing interviews and says "telly" instead of "television." Look, I'm from the Midwest—it's a TV.

Kathy eventually parlayed her material into a reality TV show, *Kathy Griffin: My Life on the D-List* for Bravo. The documentary-style show ran from 2005 to 2010 and followed

Kathy through her personal and professional struggles and exploits trying (and failing) to ascend through the Hollywood ranks. She won two Emmys for *D-List* and a legion of fans and followers enamored of her all-access, unfiltered approach to comedy.

This became Kathy's comic trademark whether she was onstage performing in any album, *Kathy Griffin: Calm Down Gurrl*. In 2013 Kathy made it into the *Guinness Book of World Records* for comedian with the most televised stand-up specials (twenty). It seems like that family move to California was not a bad call after all.

With the mighty public platform Kathy has built for herself, she's also able to throw

"*I have no filter, no limits, no class, no poise. No decorum. Just fun.*"
—KATHY GRIFFIN

one of her numerous specials or excoriating celebrity fashion choices as part of E!'s hit show, *Fashion Police*, which she appeared on for nearly seven years. Kathy's ingenuity for turning her outspoken observations into comic commentary about media and pop culture have also resulted in various awards, accolades, and milestones. Her 2008 comedy album, *For Your Consideration*, debuted on the *Billboard* 200 at number 85, making it the highest-ranked comedy album by a female comedian since 1983 (surpassing the legendary Joan Rivers). Kathy also made history when she joined an elite group of funny women to win a Grammy for her 2014

her comic bombast behind social causes close to her heart. She is a long-standing advocate for LGBTQ rights and has spoken and performed at many political events as well as organized a rally in DC in 2010 to lobby for the repeal of the military's "Don't ask, don't tell" policy. Kathy has also been active in various AIDS-related organizations, contributing to fund-raisers and awareness events.

The price Kathy pays for doing comedy her way is sometimes steep. She has been temporarily banned from late-night and daytime talk shows for her unflinching comedy and denounced by morality groups. And then there are always personal threats leveled at

Kathy through social media because, well, funny women are dangerous. Why do you think they say a comic "killed it" when she had an awesome set?

A swipe at the Trump presidency in 2017 nearly ended her career when an image from a photography shoot surfaced of Kathy holding up the disembodied mannequin head of the American president. Red state, Blue state, Green party, or card-carrying Klingon—no one was eager to defend Kathy in the name of comedy, the First Amendment, or anything else. She lost work. She lost friends. She was harassed on- and offline. Nearly a year later, she turned her experience with "haters" into "hateraid" and launched the world comedy Laugh Your Head Off Tour.

Through all of Kathy's hairpin career turns, she has remained staunchly unapologetic for someone who enjoys taking comedy to its extreme. It's all part of a job Kathy has loved doing for more than thirty years: using humor to dismantle the lines drawn around "taste" and "political correctness" while challenging notions of what is and isn't acceptable territory for funny women to rule.

MOMS MABLEY

[MARCH 19, 1894–MAY 23, 1975]

Moms Mabley was the original disruptor—African-American, woman, lesbian, and one of the first women to perform comedy solo. She brought the full force of her sly humor to national audiences during a time when African-American women were not allowed to drink from the same water fountain or attend the same schools as white people in certain places, let alone 1900s. Minstrel shows featured song-and-dance acts, comedians, and other variety acts lampooning African-American culture. Many performers playing these terrible stereotypes were white with their faces painted black, also known as "performing in blackface." On a scale of "not" to "very" racist, blackface is egregiously-terribly-horribly racist. But at the turn of the twentieth century, minstrelsy

> *"It's no disgrace to be old, but damn if it isn't inconvenient."*
> —MOMS MABLEY

have the audacity to stand up on stage and crack jokes about racism and marriage. Moms Mabley—the mother of stand-up comedy.

Born Loretta Mary Aiken, who later took the stage name Jackie "Moms" Mabley, Moms was one of sixteen children growing up in North Carolina at the turn of the twentieth century. At the age of eleven, Moms lost both her parents. Three years later, she left North Carolina for Cleveland, Ohio, where she thought she might find work with one of the traveling vaudeville-style minstrel shows.

The entertainment world was as segregated as the rest of the world in the early

and blackface were both embraced in entertainment and pop culture. Moms joined a minstrel show as a talented singer and dancer. It was there that she met and fell in love with another entertainer named Jack Mabley. The relationship crumbled, but she took the name Jackie Mabley and, later on, earned the nickname "Moms" for the supportive way she tended to fellow entertainers, men and women alike.

By the 1920s, Moms was performing with a husband-and-wife duo called Butterbeans and Susie. She made her debut at New York's famous nightclub, the Cotton Club, which hosted a huge array of African-American entertainers, such as Duke Ellington, Bessie Smith, and Lena Horne. Shortly afterward, Moms broke out on her own to establish herself as a solo performer, becoming the first woman to do what became more widely known in the 1930s and beyond as stand-up.

Adopting a funny, frumpy "housewife" persona, Moms appeared onstage in long, ugly housecoats and floppy hats. She used a bit of costuming and "show" to pass herself off as a curmudgeonly matron, just having a little chat with all the nice folks out there. That "chat" roamed over "neighborly" topics like racism, civil rights, and politics. Moms even wove numerous allusions to her lesbian identity into her act for those in the know or savvy enough to catch them. This was something that is never benign, no matter what the era, but was especially daring in the 1940s, '50s, and '60s as Moms was performing at the peak of her career.

While Moms appeared in several films in the 1940s (*Killer Diller* [1948], *Boarding House Blues* [1948]), it was always her stand-up that endeared audiences to her. In 1962 she played at the historic Carnegie Hall in New York City, which was not just significant for its size and prestige, but also because it meant that Moms had broad appeal to both white and black audiences, breaking through color barriers with her comedy. Following her Carnegie Hall show, Moms booked appearances on popular entertainment shows, like *The Ed Sullivan Show* and *The Smothers Brothers*. She recorded the first of many comedy albums (twenty in all) around this same time, *The Funniest Woman Alive*, followed by *Moms Mabley at the "UN,"* which landed on the *Billboard* Top 20.

Moms performed and recorded almost up until her death from congestive heart failure in 1975. In many ways she provided the playbook for every funny woman who came after her—one that's written from a place of courage, resilience, and reverence for laughter as one of the most powerful tools for social change.

MARGARET CHO

[DECEMBER 5, 1968–]

There wasn't anyone like Margaret Cho doing stand-up in the early 1990s: a Korean-American woman with a vocabulary filthier than a New York City sewer, slaying audiences with her raunchy material about sex, race, and gender. Margaret defied stereotypes as an outspoken Asian woman building a career in the highly competitive and often ruthless world of stand-up comedy. She also drew upon her cultural background to combat prejudice and bigotry one rapid-fire, risqué joke at a time. Basically, no one knew what to make of this fearless, young woman dominating the comedy clubs of her native San Francisco. But they could tell they were in the presence of a fresh, original voice, putting a funny, nervy spin on cultural truths that made most people too anxious to talk about. All of that was fine with Margaret—stirring the pot was something she was born to do.

Margaret's rebellious streak may have come from her mother. She resisted an arranged marriage in Korea to wed the man of her choice: a Korean joke book writer. In the Cho household, humor was literally in demand. Her parents ran a small bookstore in San Francisco, called Paperback Traffic, that happened to sit adjacent to a tiny club where Margaret would eventually perform her earliest stand-up comedy sets.

Like too many young girls, Margaret experienced her share of bullying and mean-girl behavior as a teenager. She started crafting jokes as defense and coping mechanisms; humor became her salve and saving grace. Margaret realized that being funny was a way of fitting in and, most importantly, she discovered that comedy could disarm as well as empower.

By the time she was sixteen, Margaret was regularly performing stand-up. A massive break came when she won a comedy contest with a grand prize that would make any comedian fuchsia with envy: the chance to open for stand-up icon Jerry Seinfeld. Margaret held her own as an opener for Seinfeld; he was impressed with the sophisticated way Margaret joked about her Korean heritage. Rather than play up one-dimensional stereotypes about her family or her culture, Margaret was able to spotlight racial difference in a way that reflected nuance and complexity.

Fueled by this success and the recognition it brought her, Margaret took her shot and moved to Los Angeles to further her career. She toured nationally at clubs and on college campuses, picked up minor television roles

(Margaret appeared in a failed spin-off of the popular *Golden Girls* sitcom, titled *Golden Palace*) and appeared as a regular guest on *The Arsenio Hall Show*. National audiences began to get acquainted with Margaret's brand of sharp comedy—her unique cultural viewpoint and growing popularity prompted ABC to offer Margaret a sitcom deal. The show, *All-American Girl*, would be based on Margaret's life—being the daughter of Korean-American parents who ran a bookstore in San Francisco—and her stand-up material.

was a disaster. Many felt the characters were little more than stereotypes and Margaret was subject to terrible criticism about simultaneously being "too Asian" and "not Asian enough." She was also pressured by executives to lose weight, which ultimately put her health at dire risk. The show was canceled after one season. A significant blow for Margaret, the show's cancellation contributed to a spiral into drug and alcohol addiction.

Fortunately, Margaret got sober and back to making people laugh with a clear-eyed,

> "I didn't mean to be a role model. I just speak my truth."
> —MARGARET CHO

At the time, the show was the only sitcom about an Asian family of its kind. This was 1994, when even Caucasian women on television were still playing housewives, teachers, or broken, single-gal lawyers destined to be unlucky in love (cue the sad trombone). Needless to say, roles for Asian actors and representations of Asian life and culture were almost harder to come by than shade in the desert. Despite her high hopes and hard work to make the show a success, *All-American Girl*

wickedly funny vengeance. She dealt with this turbulent time in her life with her characteristic uncompromising comedy in her 1999 one-woman show, *I'm the One That I Want* (also the title of her best-selling 2002 memoir). The show garnered critical praise—*New York* magazine awarded it Performance of the Year and *Entertainment Weekly* named it one of the year's Great Performances. What followed were a number of acclaimed stand-up specials, including *Notorious C.H.O.* (2002),

State of Emergency (2004), *Assassin* (2005), and, more recently, *Cho Dependent* (2010) and *The PsyCHO Tour* (2015). Each one covered new, deeply personal territory from Margaret's experience as a survivor of sexual abuse and her bisexual identity to bigotry and body image issues, always delivered in Margaret's unflinching, raw, outrageous voice.

Her performance stage has also become her political pulpit. Margaret has been a long-time advocate for the LGBTQ community, both onstage and off. She actively works on antibullying, antiracism, and gay rights campaigns, giving voice and support to people who feel marginalized, invisible, and challenged to find a meaningful place in society. Who better to tackle these serious, ongoing social and political issues than someone who is a living testament to the transformative power of humor, like Margaret Cho?

ALI WONG

[APRIL 19, 1982–]

There's a saying that dance impresario Ginger Rogers did everything her partner Fred Astaire did, only backwards and in high heels. We could say the same about Ali Wong: She's done everything stand-up comics have done, only as a Vietnamese-Chinese-American woman while also seven and a half months' pregnant.

Ali's 2016 Netflix comedy special, *Baby Cobra*, was filmed when she was expecting her first child. Outfitted in a form-fitting, short black-and-white dress designed to show off her considerable baby bump, Ali pulled no punches. She railed about her rapidly morphing body along with typically hands-off topics associated with impending motherhood—her sexual appetites, her actual appetites, and her ambivalence that maybe this wasn't about the miracle of life, but rather the biggest mistake of her life.

While feminine experiences are certainly not new comic territory, Ali takes audiences into uncharted waters by putting a wholly original, very graphic, and sinfully funny voice to the roller-coaster ride of reproduction. As Ali sees it, pregnancy is a theme park attraction that so many cue up for, but no one wants to talk about when they stumble bleary-eyed and dizzy from the car at the end of the ride.

Ali goes there and, like many other comic rebels, she ends up obliterating the rules to do humor her way.

Ali found her way into comedy in college, performing theater at UCLA. She became a member of the university's iconic LCC Theatre Company, a completely student-run improv troupe, where the performers wrote, directed, acted, and even handled tech for every show. The group's complete artistic freedom helped Ali explore her comedic style and sensibilities. After graduation, Ali began to branch out into stand-up. She did her first gig at a negligible space in San Francisco called the Brainwash Café, which was essentially a Laundromat/coffee bar. The one-woman show aspect of stand-up hooked her, and she soon left California to break into the comedy scene in New York.

In the city known to eat the dreams of aspiring entertainers for brunch, Ali hit the stand-up comedy circuit with a vengeance. She often played nine or more sets a night, barreling from club to club between the hours of 7 p.m. and 2 a.m., polishing her material, and refining the cutting comic voice that would unravel every stereotype of the reserved, docile Asian woman threaded through popular culture.

Her hard work paid off. Before long Ali was doing sets on *The Tonight Show, John Oliver's New York Stand-Up Show,* and *Dave Atell's Comedy Underground Show.* In 2014 Ali was hired to write for the sitcom *Fresh Off the Boat,* a groundbreaking comedy about an Asian-American family who moves from Washington, DC to Orlando in the mid-1990s to open up a cowboy-themed steak restau-

way she builds the intensity of her jokes and stories to culminate in outrageous, profanity-laced rants. It also established her as a comedian and a woman intent on challenging feminist, cultural, and industry norms.

At the opening of *Baby Cobra,* Ali makes the pointed joke that pregnant stand-up comics are more elusive than a blizzard in Cuba because—as she says sardonically—pregnant

> *"You get that anger and then you blurt out things ...that's how I write. I only write onstage. It has to come from pure emotion."*
> —ALI WONG

rant. In 2016 she took another gig as a recurring character on the show *American Housewife.* But it was Ali's bold move to do her *Baby Cobra* special that made fellow comics and fans alike agree that Ali had just vaulted herself into a whole other stratosphere of funny woman.

Baby Cobra cemented Ali's comic style—the way the tone of her voice swings between casual sweetness and caustic sarcasm; how she deftly segues from a conversational to a humorously confrontational stance; and the

comedians simply disappear. It's both a comment on the stigma surrounding pregnancy, especially for women working in entertainment, as well as a jab at the social attitudes that suggest women should give up their careers to raise kids. Lean out so far that you vanish.

Pregnancy, particularly as Ali makes hilariously, viciously clear, is disgusting, weird, biologically and socially outlandish nonsense that seems more like science fiction than a gift from Mother Nature. Ali's comedy is made up of myriad truths shared between women online or in their select groups of friends, but rarely broadcast to the masses of men and women alike, amplified through the snarky, vulgar, funny persona of a slight Asian-American woman.

Expecting her second child in 2018, Ali launched a follow-up comedy special titled *Hard Knock Wife*. Dressed in a short, clingy, leopard-print dress and bright pink glasses, Ali takes audiences on another whiplash tour through her reproductive odyssey with fetus number two. She also opens up about motherhood, bringing her characteristic bracing outlook on everything from breast-feeding to post-baby sex. Raw and unfiltered, Ali elegantly intertwines the funky realities of motherhood with their political implications. Ali's comedic sleight of hand—getting audiences to laugh at her brash honesty in talking about topics considered lewd and unpopular, while actually asking them to think about racism, sexism, and social inequality—is one of her most impressive and impactful feats as a funny woman. And if that isn't already everything, she can probably tango backwards in high heels, too.

JOAN RIVERS

[JUNE 8, 1933–SEPTEMBER 4, 2014]

If Joan Rivers had been a slightly better actress, she might have stolen Barbra Streisand's career. The two young women appeared together in the 1950s in a short (and short-lived) off-Broadway play titled *Driftwood*. Both Joan and Streisand were simply aspiring entertainers working in New York and trying to break into show business. Fortunately for Streisand, Joan realized that "dramatic" acting was not her forte. She decided to give comedy a try, and for the next seven or eight years relentlessly perfected her act on the dimly lit stages of New York comedy clubs like the Bitter End, the Gaslight, and the Duplex. It would take Joan more than a few lucky breaks to eventually become *the* Joan Rivers.

When Joan first began developing her act, there were few women performing stand-up. This alone made her novel and well-known on the comedy club circuit. Without many female stand-ups to look to for inspiration, Joan had to look to the men. One, in particular, caught her eye and ear: the infamous Lenny Bruce. Bruce flipped the comedy world on its heels with his free-form style of conversational performance that riffed on politics, religion, and pop culture. He also enjoyed a great curse word or seven, and he shared them liberally with his audience. This made him popular and scandalous, the kind of designation usually reserved for rock stars. Joan caught his act while she was still in college. She connected with Bruce's ability to make the personal deeply funny and to inject a level of candid observation to make audiences laugh at sensitive issues. Joan knew that this was the kind of comedy she wanted to do.

In the course of trying to find her own comic voice and style, Joan joined up with Chicago's Second City in 1961. The unparalleled Elaine May—whip-smart, funny, and intuitive—became one of Joan's early role models. Joan ultimately earned a reputation as one of the savviest and sharpest women comics to join the players since Elaine May. She was further inspired by Second City's intellectual atmosphere; she didn't have to dilute her jokes or insights to pander to the audience. Instead, they would just have to keep up.

Joan's first big break came in 1965 when she was booked to appear on *The Tonight Show with Johnny Carson*. Carson dominated late night and earned a reputation for making or breaking the careers of young comics. He could turn you from an unknown comedian to a household name with little more than the wave of his hand as he invited you to take a seat on the guest couch after your set. Joan nailed her first appearance on *Tonight*, earning Carson's approval. She became a regular fixture on the hottest entertainment and talk shows, like *The Dick Cavett Show*, *The Mike Douglas Show*, and *The Ed Sullivan Show*.

Throughout the 1960s and 1970s, Joan ranked as the leading lady of stand-up comedy. She sold out enormous theaters from Carnegie Hall in New York to Caesar's Pal-

ting cosmetic surgery. She openly used her "work" for comic fodder, both in terms of making fun of her looks and in owning the power of plastic surgery. Proud to go under the knife as often as needed and joking about it even more frequently, Joan shattered the shame and silence around women's relationships with beauty and body image.

Just as Joan's fiercely bombastic humor made her an iconic comedian, it also made

> *"Never be afraid to laugh at yourself. After all, you could be missing out on the joke of the century."*
>
> —JOAN RIVERS

ace in Las Vegas; she appeared on TV shows, on game shows, and in films. No matter what the setting, Joan was uncompromising in her work and her comedic voice. Her humor was biting and she deployed it on nearly every subject from marriage and relationships, to religion and politics, to celebrities, and even to herself.

Taking aim at her own physical appearance was a deep well of humor for Joan. Like Phyllis Diller, Joan did not shy away from get-

her a lightning rod for controversy. More than once, critics claimed that she went too far in making a joke about sensitive topics or in light of someone else's tragedy or misfortune. Joan swatted back as if her detractors were nothing more than hornets hovering around a picnic lunch. For Joan, nothing was off-limits and even less was untouchable. Everything that passed through her orbit was filtered for its humor potential. "Can we talk?" was Joan's signature phrase and prompt for audiences to ready themselves for turbulence. She elevated the "tell it like it is" delivery to a weaponized art form that would ripple out into the performance styles of Kathy Griffin, Chelsea Handler, Michelle Wolf, and countless others.

By the late 1980s, Joan had added a new gig to her flourishing resume: daytime talk show host. *The Joan Rivers Show* premiered in 1989 and featured a mix of celebrity and oddball guests, all revolving around Joan's stream of consciousness–type humorous riffing and snarky commentary. Joan eventually won a Daytime Emmy for her show, which ran for five seasons and showcased her polish as a stand-up as well as her ability to deliver off-the-cuff jokes on the spot. In many ways, *The Joan Rivers Show* (a title that could accurately sum up her entire life) primed audiences for some of her best-known work in the 1990s and early 2000s: hosting and serving as a commentator on awards shows.

In 1994, Joan joined forces with her daughter Melissa to cohost the first Golden Globes preawards show for E!. In those prehistoric days before the internet, people had to read magazines or newspapers to find out the "inside" scoop on awards shows. Joan and Melissa revolutionized entertainment media by covering the stars as they arrived for the event in a truly unforgettable Joan Rivers kind of way: with one-on-one interactions that were heavy on the sarcasm and unscripted, thinly disguised insults. Before long, other networks dispatched their own teams of infotainment reporters to the red carpet of the big awards shows, but there was only one Joan Rivers. Hers was the only show with an "anything could happen" factor. And Joan never disappointed.

By the first decade of the millennium, just several years before her untimely death in 2014, Joan had seemingly accomplished it all: She toured avidly doing stand-up; appeared in numerous TV shows and film projects; wrote several best-selling books (her twelfth book, *Diary of a Mad Diva* was published two months before she unexpectedly passed away); had a documentary made about her life and career (*Joan Rivers: A Piece of Work*); and had launched her own online talk show on YouTube, titled *In Bed with Joan*, that featured Joan lounging in bed with a celebrity friend or guest and chatting conversationally about work, relationships, politics, or whatever came tumbling out of Joan's razor-sharp mind. What was left to tackle? Wrong question for Joan. At eighty-one years young, Joan saw an endless road paved by comedy stretching in all directions. Much of it Joan carved out herself with her staggering accomplishments, her unyielding drive to do the work she loved, and her unapologetic, game-changing comic style.

While Joan's work and life were ultimately cut short, the path she forged remains well-worn by the countless women who followed in her footsteps and continue her work. Joan remains a legendary, pioneering comedian whose no-holds-barred style of self-deprecating insult comedy and Teflon resilience made her into an idol and role model for generations of funny women.

ILANA GLAZER
[APRIL 12, 1987–]

ABBI JACOBSON
[FEBRUARY 1, 1984–]

Lucy and Ethel, Mary and Rhoda, Laverne and Shirley—please make room for two new legendary BFFs: Ilana Glazer and Abbi Jacobson. Ilana and Abbi are two real-life friends playing super besties on their hit show *Broad City*. The girls portray multifaceted, relatable young women whose differences enrich their friendship and make their exploits bruisingly funny. Ilana is a free-spirited, sexually voracious feminist who thinks nothing of to keep their hard-won dignity and ample supply of pot intact.

After Abbi graduated from the Maryland Institute College of Art in Baltimore, she relocated to New York to study acting at the prestigious Atlantic Acting School (founded by William H. Macy and David Mamet). For Abbi, the school was not a great fit with her artistic sensibilities or style. She dropped out and took a retail job to make ends meet while she figured

> *"You have to be your own cause. Even if it feels lame and stupid sometimes, define your voice and share it. That's your purpose."*
> —ILANA GLAZER

breaking into silly voices and accents whenever the mood strikes her—at work, during sex, in a crowded restaurant. Abbi is an aspiring artist/illustrator whose good deeds almost always go punished. The two friends challenge each other as much as they look out for, support, and truly love one another. The "broads" of *Broad City* are not only real, but are equally and individually outrageously funny as two ordinary, young women stumbling through life with all its petty humiliations, just trying out her next move. A roommate suggested she check out what was going on at the Upright Citizens Brigade (UCB). Abbi was floored by the improvisers she saw onstage; never before had she seen that type of live, spontaneously generated kind of comedy. She signed up for classes and began learning the improv ropes. A year later she joined an improv group that met regularly outside of classes to hone their comedy chops. That's where she first met fellow UCB player, Ilana Glazer.

Ilana grew up on Long Island, where she and her older brother, Eliot, regularly goofed around by making up silly songs, skits, and shows. When Eliot headed to Manhattan to attend NYU, Ilana followed. She applied for early admission and was accepted. Though she was a psychology major, Ilana was more interested in pursuing comedy, like Eliot. He suggested they take classes together at UCB. They ended up forming an improv team who practiced and rehearsed together off-hours and eventually drew Abbi into Ilana's orbit. The young women found an organic, comic chemistry between them that made them a hilarious duo. They also shared similar struggles trying to get cast for UCB shows amid steep competition. Finally, Ilana and Abbi understood what other powerhouse women of comedy before them realized: Don't wait around for someone to give you permission to make the comedy you want to see in the world—go make it yourself.

The pair decided to mine their own lives and experiences as New Yorkers to write, film, produce, and star in a series of webisodes they called *Broad City*. The show landed on the radar of UCB cofounder Amy Poehler, who became a fan—the ultimate comedy nerd's fantasy. As Abbi and Ilana prepared to film their last episode, they dreamed of getting a celebrity to make an appearance. A UCB instructor put the girls in touch with Amy who agreed to make a cameo—the ultimate comedy nerd fantasy *come true*. Amy's involvement changed everything on several fronts: It made the show's YouTube traffic spike off the charts, bringing the girls a huge amount of recognition and it gave them a powerful ally in Amy. The girls pitched her the idea of serving as executive producer of a TV version of the show and then she helped them land a development deal with Comedy Central. Ilana and Abbi released their smart, sly buddy sitcom to the masses in January 2014.

Broad City is a fresh, very funny recasting of the kind of sitcom that revolves around the exploits of two female best friends. Part of what has won the show its legion of fans is the authenticity that Abbi and Ilana bring to their characters. They aren't poised, sophisticated, glamorous, or entitled. They are doing the best they can to get by and score the occasional victory for the average person, poking fun at the curveballs life hurls at them along the way. The other element that puts *Broad City* in a class of its own is the topics explored on the show. It's a slice of real life, served up by Abbi and Ilana, which means that nearly everything is in play as comic fodder—drug culture, sexuality, feminism, religion, politics, race, and even deeply specific feminine experiences, like unexpectedly getting your period on an international flight. Even the most mundane happenings get the *Broad City* treatment—Abbi and Ilana skyping each other while using the bathroom—showing that if it has the potential to be funny, it's fair game.

Apart from the show, Ilana and Abbi are involved in individual projects. Abbi has published two adult coloring books, as well as *Carry This Book*, which shows glimpses of the imagined stuff carried by real and fictional celebrities. She continues to develop her art and illustrations as well as taking on various film and TV projects, including working as a writer for the TV series version of *A League of Their Own*. Ilana has branched out into film (*Rough Night*, costarring Kate McKinnon and Zoë Kravitz) and toured as a stand-up. No matter what else this funny, bestie super-duo has planned, one thing is certain: Their brand of silly, savvy feminist humor is a game-changer for all women.

"Everybody has will—you just have to gather it. And I guess you choose where your inspiration comes from and give yourself that permission."
—ABBI JACOBSON

SANDRA BERNHARD

[JUNE 6, 1955–]

Sandra Bernhard was eight years old, attending her cousin Bernice's bat mitzvah, when something happened that set her on the path that would become her life's work. The band was ruining one of Sandra's favorite show tunes, "Hello Dolly!" So she did the only thing that seemed reasonable to her: She rushed up onstage and demanded the microphone from the bandleader. The bandleader waved her off the way you'd wave off a seagull making for your half-way actor. Her family had moved from Michigan to Arizona when Sandra was ten. After graduating from high school, she spent some time figuring out her path to performance. New York was the logical choice for a career in theater, but she didn't want to be that far away from home. She settled on LA, getting involved in the entertainment scene as a singer before eventually trying stand-up. Sandra did her first five minutes of material at a club in Beverly Hills called Ye Little Club.

"Power is having a very clear point of view about what's important in your life."

— SANDRA BERNHARD

eaten sandwich. Bernice shouted out to let her cousin sing the song and Sandra happily obliged. She set the crowd on its feet, belting out a showstopping version of the Broadway classic as if she were shooting for her Tony Award in front of a theater full of people. As the expression goes, "A star was born," except, in this case, it was more like a star exploded and became an unstoppable comet named Sandra Bernhard.

Sandra fell in love with musical theater as a kid, banking on one day becoming a Broad-

The jokes were pretty basic, mostly because Sandra never saw herself as a typical comedian. Instead, she was drawn to the sensibilities and styles of women like Bette Midler and Lily Tomlin, who did characters, monologues, and songs. She was fortunate enough to strike up a friendship with two comedians she met through the clubs—Paul Mooney and Lotus Weinstock—who showed her the ropes, gave her support, and helped her work on material.

That material helped give her a whole new direction. Brash, unfiltered, and unafraid to unleash her strong opinions on audiences, Sandra trained an unflinching gaze on the hypocrisy of celebrities, sexism, and conservative politics. She also covered material that was more personal—religion, sexuality, feminism—with the same humor that sliced deeply without apology. That was perhaps one of the most striking aspects about Sandra and what made her stand out: She performed with a fearsome chemistry of self-possession, self-confidence, and self-love. Unlike her well-respected and admired predecessors, such as Joan Rivers and Phyllis Diller, Sandra was not interested in using self-deprecating humor to get a laugh. Instead, she wanted to extend the political and philosophical real estate for women hard won by second wave feminism. Sandra knew there was power in being yourself, in standing up for what you believe in, and in allowing others to see your authenticity. It's a belief that formed the cornerstone of her entire comedy career, as it was starting to take off in the early 1980s and continues to drive her unique brand of performance and humor today.

One of Sandra's first big career breaks came when she was cast in Martin Scorsese's 1983 dark satire, *The King of Comedy*. In it, Sandra played Masha, an obsessed stalker/ super-fan of a renowned comedian named Jerry Langford, played by real comic Jerry Lewis. She won a National Society of Film Critics Award for Best Supporting Actress and began to appear regularly on *Late Night with David Letterman* as well as on other popular talk and late-night shows.

She also toured widely throughout the 1980s and again in the late 1990s with several critically acclaimed one-woman shows that were truly all her own. They mixed Sandra's signature stand-up with cabaret-type performance of songs, poetry, monologues, and even guest musicians and performers. Her 1998 show, *I'm Still Here . . . Damn It!* was recorded for a comedy album and film. It featured Sandra delivering her typical scathing observations on celebrity culture and modern life as well as performing rap, poetry, a short set of rock/pop tunes, and even a bit of striptease. Sandra Bernhard: an uncompromising, innovative funny woman who smashes barriers for breakfast.

Sandra brought this same kind of fresh originality to the small screen when she was cast as a recurring character on the popular sitcom *Roseanne*, starring fellow comedian Roseanne Barr. Sandra played Nancy Bartlett, an openly gay character in more than thirty episodes between 1991 and 1997. It was the first recurring lesbian character on a network sitcom. Sandra developed the character from material in her shows in which she candidly talked about her own fluid sexuality. She portrayed a complex, diverse character who was not a stereotype or the punch line of cheap humor. Her characterization of Nancy went a long way toward raising visibility about the LGBTQ community, something that Sandra has always passionately supported.

Between appearing on many TV shows and in films, Sandra has also written three best-selling books and recorded several music and comedy albums. She currently hosts the radio show, *Sandyland*, broadcast on SiriusXM's Radio Andy channel. On the show, Sandra sits down with celebrities and public figures for candid, interesting, funny conversations about life, work, relationships, and just about everything in between.

Sandra Bernhard doesn't just redraw the lines on the comedy map, she ditches it altogether to go wherever her creative passions take her. Just like one of her live shows, Sandra resists categorization—personally and professionally—and she wouldn't have it any other way.

MAGNIFICENT, MARVELOUS, MIGHTY MISFITS

MELISSA McCARTHY

AMY SEDARIS

KRISTEN WIIG

MINDY KALING

MARIE DRESSLER

KRISTEN SCHAAL
MARIA BAMFORD

FANNY BRICE

ELLEN DeGENERES

TRACEY ULLMAN

PHYLLIS DILLER

It's a mighty thing to rock what makes you different and unique. No one understands that better than the women who tap into their outlier status to make us laugh and, in doing so, help us all feel like we're not the only weirdos on the planet. Funny women proudly rocking their misfit labels are the ones who grace us with some of the most inventive, novel, and exciting kinds of comedy. They see the world from an off-kilter perspective that draws them to the kinds of topics, ideas, and approaches to humor that other people have tossed aside as too bizarre or strange. It's kind of that "One woman's comedy junk is another woman's comedy treasure" attitude.

By showing up as their most genuine selves, by turning their unconventional looks or physiques or comic voices and sensibilities into their mightiest assets, these women invite and inspire more diverse femininity. They undermine the assumption that women should conform to some kind of arbitrary and unrealistic set of ideals to be considered successful, desirable, or marketable. They do not have time for that nonsense, thank you very much. These women are too busy killing it on the regular to concern themselves with anything that slows them down or keeps them from hurtling into the comedy stratosphere.

EXTRA EXTRAORDINAIRES: Lisa Kudrow · Bette Midler · Joann Worley · Rosie O'Donnell · Imogene Coca · May Irwin · Sophie Tucker · Judy Tenuta · Garfunkel & Oates · Geri Jewell · Zooey Deschanel · Phoebe Mary Waller-Bridge · Cloris Leachman

MELISSA McCARTHY

[AUGUST 26, 1970–]

From her earliest role as the klutzy Sookie St. James on *Gilmore Girls* to reprising Chris Farley's bombastic Matt Foley character for *SNL*'s fortieth anniversary special, Melissa McCarthy has mastered the art of the scene steal with her entire body. On TV shows and in movies, she crashes through tables, whips herself into a frenzy on the dance floor, dangles precariously from the leg of an out-of-control helicopter, and gets into hilarious smackdowns with perps and PTA moms alike. She is pure comic kinetic energy, forging a path for herself in comedy powered by joyful anarchy and sheer tenacity.

As she was starting out in Hollywood, Melissa routinely ran up against critics who told her that no one wanted to see a plus-size woman on the big screen, even if that woman was taking pratfalls and trading killer one-liners with the best of them. Notice that these same people were not telling Chris Farley, Kevin James, or John Candy to drop a few pounds or make themselves attractive to be more "camera-ready." This is what's known as a lousy double standard that stinks worse than the inside of Serena Williams's tennis sneakers after the US Open. Lucky for us, Melissa has torpedoed that double standard, getting the last laugh by making comedy where she can be her most real, audacious, irrepressible self.

Melissa grew up in a large Catholic family on a working farm in Plainfield, Illinois. When she wasn't doing her chores, she was watching and worshipping the funny folks on *Saturday Night Live* or ambushing her mother by entertaining her with silly made-up songs. It was Melissa's version of dinner and a show, minus the dinner, for one of her biggest fans already. Melissa's mother and father heaped endless support and encouragement upon her, no matter what hobbies, sports, or interests caught her attention. Their advocacy went a long way toward helping to build Melissa's self-confidence and passion for performing.

Melissa's natural inclination to crack jokes and make people laugh in high school fueled her desire to pursue a career in comedy. After graduating from Joliet Catholic Academy, she moved to New York to try her hand at stand-up comedy. While performing at area clubs, Melissa studied acting at the Actors Studio before ultimately deciding to relocate to Los Angeles in the mid-1990s to seek out film and television work. In LA, Melissa discovered the comedy training equivalent of West Point: the Groundlings.

Melissa thrived in this highly competitive comedy theater. She readily advanced through the theater's five training levels—many students are asked to repeat their levels until the instructor feels they're ready to move on—to earn a place performing in the Main Company, also known as becoming an official Groundling. Performers making Groundling status can remain there indefinitely or, as is usually the case, until they go on to star in by critics and fans. Melissa and Gardell earned great praise for their portrayals of relatable characters who—despite falling outside the narrow (not to mention idiotic) idealized body norms for television—played against stereotypes. It was a refreshing and important shift to see a woman like Melissa bring a character to life who was more than the sum of her physical parts. She went on to win an Emmy for Outstanding Lead Actress in a Comedy

> "I never felt like I needed to change . . .
> I've always thought, if you want someone different,
> pick somebody else."
> —MELISSA McCARTHY

films, TV shows, or lend their crazy, funny talents to some other amazing project. Melissa spent nine years as a Groundling. She found a hugely talented group of people to work with, which included her future husband, Ben Falcone, and left the troupe in 2000 for the part of Sookie on *Gilmore Girls*.

The popularity of Melissa's character on *Gilmore Girls* led to a starring role in the sitcom *Mike and Molly* with comedian Billy Gardell. Overall, the show was positively received Series and a People's Choice Award for her portrayal of Molly. But it was in her no-holds-barred film comedies that Melissa dazzled the most, breaking and rewriting the rules for unconventional funny women onscreen.

Anyone who saw Paul Feig's *Bridesmaids* could not have missed Melissa as a major standout in the already powerhouse ensemble of comedians Kristen Wiig, Ellie Kemper, Maya Rudolph, Rose Byrne, and Wendi McLendon-Covey. Melissa's Megan is a lovingly crass, scandalously uninhibited woman whose cockiness is equal parts enviable and empowering. Whether she's flagrantly and cheekily propositioning a stranger on a plane ("Why don't we go back to the restroom and not rest?") or making the disgusting effects of volcanic food poisoning unbearably funny, Melissa's performance in *Bridesmaids* put her in a class of women comics who embraced their diversity as an extraordinary—and in this case, extraordinarily funny—asset, rather than an industry liability.

Melissa deployed her signature joyfully bombastic approach to comedy in a run of successful films following *Bridesmaids*—*Identity Thief* (2013), *The Heat* (2013), *The Boss* (2106), and *Ghostbusters* (2016), to name just a few. In each, Melissa plays her offbeat, brash characters with swagger and self-love. Even when they appear to be making fools of themselves—on the dance floor, at a cosmetic counter, or rocking a greasy fast food paper bag mask to rob said fast food joint—Melissa's characters are never the punch line. Instead, she owns her characters' comic humiliation, making it all a source of pride, rather than shame.

When she's not dominating on the big and small screens—Melissa's guest appearances on *Saturday Night Live* in 2016 as the ornery, electronic-podium-driving former White House press secretary Sean Spicer became an instant comedy classic—Melissa runs her own production company, On the Day, with her husband, and works on an evolving fashion line for plus-size women called Melissa McCarthy Seven7.

Melissa demonstrates over and over again that getting overlooked for a part or project because you don't fit into a certain kind of comedic or feminine "type" might be discouraging, but it can really be a powerful gift. For Melissa, it means getting to make her own set of rules, and driving laughter in ways that are surprising, novel, and ultimately energizing to another generation of funny, unconventional women, ready to unleash their comedy genius on the world.

AMY SEDARIS

[MARCH 29, 1961–]

magine shopping at a grocery store and hearing the voice of an employee come over the loudspeaker making an announcement like this: "Good afternoon, shoppers! Today we've got a great special on Chocolate-Coated Oatie O's, two for $1.89 and a coupon inside for half off your next root canal!" That would have been the twisted humor of a sixteen-year-old Amy Sedaris. Okay, maybe Amy didn't make this exact announcement, but when she worked at the local Winn-Dixie supermarket in her hometown of Raleigh, North Carolina, she was known to hijack the PA system to have a bit of "on-air" fun. Though the management did not appreciate Amy's silly genius, clowning around at the market amused her coworkers and, even more importantly, made herself crack up. To Amy, it was just part of her relentless DIY approach to comedy: If it doesn't exist, make it yourself.

Amy is one of five siblings, including her well-known brother, humor writer David Sedaris. Living in a big family, there was always competition for more than just the last scoop of mashed potatoes. Amy's mother was a strong woman with a terrific sense of humor, who had a knack for delivering withering sarcasm and telling wonderful, funny stories. Amy wasn't the only one angling for her mother's time and attention, but she took the most creative route to get it. She dressed up in weird costumes and wore crazy wigs that often did the trick to get her mother to notice her in the midst of the sibling melee. She also developed a talent for impersonating both her parents, which must have made for some pretty entertaining Thanksgiving dinners.

After graduating from high school, Amy and her mother briefly went into business running a small bakery together. Amy eventually decided it was time for a change and followed David to Chicago. There she found a city brimming with theater and comedy of all kinds—Shakespearean drama; huge musicals making their way to Broadway; funky, indie theater staged in the basements of dive bars and industrial lofts; stand-up comedy clubs; and sketch and improv theaters. People who wanted to play—this was Amy's kind of town. No surprise at all that Amy found her way to a group of quirky, kindred spirits when she eventually enrolled at Second City.

Amy joined a group of performers testing the limits (and sometimes hurtling right over them) of humor. Her fellow players included the strange and talented minds of Stephen Colbert (*The Late Show with*

Stephen Colbert), Steve Carell (*The Office*), Nia Vardalos (*My Big Fat Greek Wedding*), and Paul Dinello (*Strangers with Candy*). They shared comic sensibilities while finding the funny in sub- and countercultures, in dark or unusual scenarios, and in turning the misfits of these scenes into heroes. While writing and performing for Second City, as well as cowriting several plays with her brother, Amy more fully explored her love for all kinds of characters. But her favorite creations were the unusual outliers—individuals seen as freaks, losers, oddballs, and eccentrics. For Amy, these kinds of characters were the most interesting, complicated, and ultimately, lovable. Her character work in the Chicago comedy scene laid the foundation for one of her best-known weirdos—a middle-aged high school student named Jerri Blank who would dominate a cult-comedy show Amy helped to create with Dinello, titled *Strangers with Candy*.

Strangers was both a parody and a satire of television shows about high school and adolescent culture stretched to the extreme. The show tracked the exploits of Jerri Blank, a forty-six-year-old woman returning to resume her freshman year of high school. Jerri ran away from home as a teen to live a life as a notorious "user, boozer, and loser," becoming, among many things, an addict, a sex worker, and a thief. To play Jerri, Amy transformed herself into an unattractive middle-aged woman with a retro upswept hairdo, a pronounced overbite, and a wardrobe of turtlenecks and sleeveless knit sweaters that made her look like a walking page out of a Sears catalogue from 1978. Each episode found Jerri trying to navigate the bizarre yet familiar terrain of high school as an older woman with a ton of baggage and life experience. Amy played Jerri as a proud disaster who loves and values herself as a person and a woman. In Jerri, Amy brushed aside ideas about traditional beauty to make the case that femininity, beauty, and even sexiness come from within: Turtlenecks or scoop necks, beauty is what you believe it to be.

Strangers with Candy aired from 1999 to 2000 and even inspired a prequel movie with original cast members in 2005. Though Amy retired Jerri's overbite and wig, she has continued to lend her endearingly skewed comic sensibilities to a slew of projects for film, television, publishing, and the web. Amy combined her love for comedy and crafting culture with two books, *I Like You: Hospitality Under the Influence* (2008) and *Simple Times: Crafts for Poor People* (2010). Both are brilliantly cheeky riffs on the upscale crafting craze sparked by Etsy and Pinterest, except with less French lace and more pipe cleaners, seashells, and empty toilet paper rolls. Amy's enthusiasm for the humor potential of the DIY industry morphed into the 2017 television series, *At Home with Amy Sedaris.*

At Home borrows from shows like *Martha Stewart Living, The Barefoot Contessa,* and *The Frugal Gourmet,* put through the delirious blender of Amy's keen, offbeat comedy. Amy plays herself on this satirical cooking, design, craft, and life-skills type of home show that is based on different weekly themes, such as "Cooking for One" or "Hosting the Holidays." Amy's *At Home* is not a dig at the ridiculousness of perfect homemaking; it's a celebration of doing domestic your way, unapologetically, with as much fun as possible.

Amy Sedaris is the kind of funny woman who does comedy with open arms. She embraces the kooks, outcasts, and endearing aberrations living just under the surface of herself, and in the process encourages the rest of us to celebrate our own lovable inner weirdos.

"There's humor in everything. There's gotta be humor in everything."

—AMY SEDARIS

KRISTEN WIIG

[AUGUST 22, 1973–]

An introvert is asked to give a speech and laughter ensues. At first it sounds like one of the kooky characters that Kristen Wiig has brought to life, except it isn't. It's Kristen herself. The same person who rose to fame on *Saturday Night Live*, with characters like the loud, obnoxious Target Lady and the inexhaustible "one-upper" Penelope, was once terrified of public speaking, turning into a puddle at the thought of doing anything as getting her degree, she stayed in Arizona and landed a job with a plastic surgery clinic, sketching drawings of people's post-surgery images. (This also sounds like the premise of a Kristen Wiig character.) However, the day before she was due to start work, Kristen took a hard look at this career choice and realized: Nope. The time she spent in acting class had made a more profound impression on her than she realized, and sketching the outlines

> "Don't become something just because someone else wants you to, or because it's easy; you won't be happy. You have to do what you really, really, really, really want to do, even if it scares the shit out of you."
>
> —KRISTEN WIIG

risky and nerve-racking as performing live onstage every week for millions of viewers. Thankfully, Kristen got over it.

Kristen had her sights set on becoming a graphic artist when she enrolled at the University of Arizona, but an acting class she took to fulfill a course requirement put her on a different path. Surprisingly enough to the naturally shy girl from Rochester, New York, Kristen found she really enjoyed the class. After of people's newly perfected noses, eyelids, and lips was not where she wanted to spend the next ten years of her life (or even the next ten minutes). The next day, instead of punching in at the plastic surgery clinic, Kristen punched the gas pedal and sped off toward a new life in Los Angeles.

In LA, Kristen became one of the many hopefuls working day jobs, auditioning, and trying like mad for that big or even mediumish break. She had zero experience and even less of a plan on how to make that break happen, but people have achieved greater feats with little more than a few notes scratched on the back of a napkin and a lot of determination. And while the shiny, star-making part in someone's mega movie or hit TV show did not happen for Kristen, it turns out that something better did: the Groundlings. A friend took her to see a show at the famous improv and sketch theater and the ground beneath Kristen Wiig's feet shifted (not literally, even though it is California and that can actually happen when you live along major fault lines). Making it up as you went along appealed to Kristen much more than the intimidation of having to deliver lines from a script. She auditioned immediately and began taking classes at the theater.

Four to five months after becoming a member of the company, Kristen got word that Lorne Michaels was interested in having her audition for *SNL*. He had seen a tape of material that Kristen's manager had sent over to the producers, so she flew to New York to audition. The audition process involved doing a rigidly timed five-minute set, consisting of five impressions and three characters. Like so many of her predecessors, Kristen would perform in a darkened studio for a group of shadowy figures who may or may not be people you've spent your entire life idolizing. Performing brain surgery on the pope is less stressful than an *SNL* audition. Kristen gave it her all. They asked her for a second audition and several months later they offered her a job. Big break achievement unlocked!

From then on, oddball characters came parading out of Kristen across the soundstage of studio 8-H and into audiences' lives: the creepy, borderline psychotic elementary-school girl Gilly; the delusional actress Mindy Gracin; the hypersexual Shana, whose attempts at cool seduction always resulted in something disgusting, like spitting out food or coughing up phlegm; and the cantankerous, never-satisfied movie critic, Aunt Linda. Kristen played all these characters with an inflated sense of self-importance and a high degree of self-worth. Her fictional personas embraced their weirdness, which became their source of power and laughter.

Kristen spent seven years on *SNL*, earning several Emmy nominations, before branching out into film. She starred in and cowrote, with fellow Groundling alum Annie Mumolo, the 2011 breakout comedy hit, *Bridesmaids*. Cast alongside an enormously talented ensemble of funny women, Kristen played Annie Walker, a down-on-her-luck baker whose best friend, Lillian, asks her to be her maid of honor. Annie throws herself into her duties, but only succeeds in making one epically funny catastrophic choice after another. She's the misfit character all women can relate to—the one who tries to mask her insecurities while unsuccessfully triaging a life that has gone off the rails. Kristen's earnestness as someone doing the best she can, even when that actually means the worst she can, lets us laugh at Annie as someone flawed and sympathetic.

Kristen continues to rack up film credits—*Ghostbusters* (2016), *Despicable Me* (2010), *Friends with Kids* (2011), and *Wonder Woman 2* (2019), realizing characters rooted in the joy and humorous struggle of nonconformity. Though many of Kristen's creations seem a little like they might have arrived here from another planet, they let a certain amount of vulnerability leak through the cracks in their quirkiness. Kristen ultimately uses comedy to connect women to the cringey, awkward, incomprehensible parts of ourselves that society tries to make us edit out in a quest for perfection. Instead, Kristen relishes the humor and humanity of imperfection; the result is a relatable everywoman who celebrates living proudly as a stranger in a strange land.

MINDY KALING

[JUNE 24, 1979–]

Even in her own family, Mindy Kaling (born Vera Chokalingam) was something of a happy outlier. Her Indian parents met while her architect father was working on the new wing of a hospital where her mother was practicing obstetrics and gynecology. Science, medicine, architecture, and engineering were the preferred fields of Mindy's extended family. There was not one comedian in the clan until, that is, Mindy came along.

Mindy's comedic spark might have become lit the day her parents decided they wanted to give their daughter a more common, cute American name to go with her new life in the United States. As it turned out, Mindy's parents were big fans of the 1970s TV show *Mork & Mindy*. In what might have become a self-fulfilling prophecy, their daughter, whom they named after a sitcom character, would go on to create and star in a sitcom of her own.

Mindy credits her mother, who passed away from pancreatic cancer in 2012, with instilling in her a healthy sense of humor. Mindy's mother possessed a sharp wit and was beloved by her patients for making them laugh—an invaluable skill for someone helping women navigate what could often feel like a slalom skiing course of the reproduction experience. It also didn't hurt that Mindy spent a lot of her childhood and teen years immersed in popular TV comedies of the late '80s and early 1990s, like *Kids in the Hall*, *Mad TV*, and *Saturday Night Live*. Mindy not only fan-girled these shows, but she studied them like a botanist studying a new strain of plant. For Mindy, comedy was always serious business.

Born and raised in Cambridge, Massachusetts, Mindy attended Dartmouth College in Hanover, New Hampshire, where she studied playwriting. She often stood out against her predominantly white classmates, but quickly found humor as a powerful equalizer. She joined the school's improv troupe, the Dog Day Players, drew the comic strip called *Badly Drawn Girl* for the school's newspaper, and wrote a humor column for the *Dartmouth Jack-o-Lantern*, the campus's humor magazine.

After graduation, Mindy moved to Brooklyn with two other college friends to break into the New York entertainment scene. She took a day job as a production assistant on the show *Crossing Over* and dabbled in stand-up comedy. After the fifth or sixth club emcee made the same lame joke about her hard-to-pronounce name, Mindy knew she was going to have to help people see her as a funny person above all else, not an "Indian woman who also happened to be funny." Keeping "Mindy," she borrowed "Kaling" from the middle, most discernable part of her last name, and Mindy Kaling became the new funny stand-up making the comedy club rounds.

Sometimes the most fantastic opportunities seem to drop into your life out of nowhere,

Matt Damon—the pair behind the 1997 Oscar hit *Good Will Hunting*. Their riffing turned to writing, which turned into a short play: *Matt & Ben*, starring Mindy as Ben Affleck and Withers as Matt Damon. The play's premise involved Matt and Ben working on a screenplay adaptation of J. D. Salinger's novel *The Catcher in the Rye* when the script for *Good Will Hunting* inexplicably falls from the ceiling of their apartment. The rest of the pleasantly absurd show revolved around the

"Write your own part. It is the only way I've gotten anywhere."

— MINDY KALING

like a sack of unmarked hundred-dollar bills dumped from a plane (or something else equally as fantastic and slightly more realistic). For Mindy, the startling success of a play she wrote, titled *Matt & Ben*, was one such marvelous and completely unexpected happening.

In 2002, Mindy and her roommate, Brenda Withers (also her best friend from Dartmouth), found themselves goofing around with a funny idea about what it was like to be superstar besties Ben Affleck and

boys' friendship, made even sillier by Mindy and Withers satirizing the dude-love between the two.

Something that started out as pure fun for Mindy and Withers got them some serious recognition: *Matt & Ben* earned critical acclaim at the New York International Fringe Festival and was hailed by *Time* magazine as one of the "Top Ten Theatrical Events of the Year." More importantly, the play put Mindy on the radar of Greg Daniels, a comedy writer and director working on adapting the UK version of the Ricky Gervais show, *The Office*, for American television. Two months after Daniels caught a performance of *Matt & Ben*, he offered Mindy a job writing for *The Office*.

When Mindy joined *The Office*, she was the only woman on a writing staff of eight. Rather than trying to conform, Mindy took the opportunity to stand out and let her diversity inform her quick-witted, snark-laced kind of humor in the writing room. The rest of the team were so taken with Mindy's fresh, sharp comedy that they created an exaggerated version of Mindy to become part of the show. The result was the earnestly shallow, materialistic, pop culture–obsessed, sweetly clueless character Kelly Kapoor.

Over the course of her time with *The Office*, Mindy wrote, performed, directed, and earned an executive producer credit. Several of her episodes became stand-outs as beloved "fan favorites," such as "The Injury," where Michael Scott burns his foot on a George Foreman grill and "Niagara" where workplace sweethearts Jim and Pam eventually tie the knot. That particular episode won Mindy an Emmy nomination for cowriting, along with Daniels. But it was her portrayal of Kelly that made one of the biggest impacts on both audiences and Mindy herself. Rather than mar-ginalizing Kelly as a "token" kind of ethnic character, Mindy played Kelly as another one of the sweetly dysfunctional office gang who also happens to be Indian. Mindy carved out a new space on television for a character like Kelly, who challenged audiences to see her as a dynamic woman who had both merits and flaws, instead of simply a character marked by her difference. It was Mindy's way of reversing the trend she noticed growing up watching TV: No one onscreen looked like her or her family.

Mindy continued to remedy that oversight following her time on *The Office* with a series of her own, *The Mindy Project*. It starred Mindy as the character Mindy Lahiri, an accomplished OB/GYN (inspired by her mother) navigating life, career, and relationships alongside a cast of misfit coworkers and friends. Mindy Lahiri is a successful career woman who celebrates every aspect of who she is—a hopeless romantic obsessed with romcoms, an ambitious professional who is also sometimes insecure and a bit of a mess, and a sexually confident person, proud to be an Indian woman who loves her body exactly as it is. And she's funny, too. Mindy Kaling gave viewers a diverse female character who wasn't just an object of curiosity, but rather an interesting, engaging, dynamic woman to aspire to.

In the midst of evolving her television and film career (she starred in 2018's fantasy film hit *A Wrinkle in Time* and the all-female heist flick, *Oceans 8*), Mindy has kept true to her writing roots. In 2011 she penned the *New York Times* best-selling memoir, *Is Everyone Hanging Out without Me? (And Other Concerns)*, and the 2015 follow-up, *Why Not Me?*

In her books as well as in the characters she's developed elsewhere, Mindy shines through as a real woman, using her sharp wit and humorous savvy to soothe the chafe that often comes with feeling like an outsider or a misfit. There's strength and power in letting the things that make you unique be your greatest resources or, as Mindy has shown us: Sometimes the best way to belong is by having the courage to let the world see you as your funniest, oddest, truest self.

MARIE DRESSLER

[NOVEMBER 9, 1868–JULY 28, 1934]

Some fourteen-year-olds assert their independence by working summer jobs or getting regrettable body piercings. When Marie Dressler was fourteen, she left her family in Ohio, where they had settled after leaving Ontario, to pursue a life in the theater. This was 1878—not exactly a time when you could just call an Uber and ride out of town. Also, the whole "getting a job in the theater" thing was not as straightforward as showing up in New York or Chicago ready to audition your heart out. In the 1800s, theater was an economically and morally dubious "profession," especially for women. In addition to traveling around the country with a troupe for little to no money, many people thought "actress" was polite code for "prostitute." Not a ringing endorsement for young Marie. However, she knew the risks and cared not a whit. Marie was meant for the stage, especially if it meant getting people to laugh.

Marie Dressler was born in 1868 as Leila Marie Koerber in the sleepy town of Cobourg, Ontario. Her father possessed a terrible temper and little patience, but he did have a gift for teaching the violin and piano. Marie was five when she got her first shot at the spotlight. Marie's mother organized something called a Valentine's tableau vivant for the local Episcopal church. Tableaus were specific kinds of nineteenth-century amusements that involved people creating living pictures. Dressed in ornate costumes, people gathered in parlors or church halls and re-created iconic scenes from history, Greek antiquity, or even the Bible. Really. You have not lived until you've spent a Saturday evening watching your friends and neighbors assemble themselves in the image of Washington crossing the Delaware in your living room. Really, again. This was a hot-night-of-fun-time for the local folks.

Marie played Cupid in the tableau, her mother outfitting her in nothing but a strategically placed bow and arrow (no judgment because it was "theater"), and setting the plump Marie atop a pedestal. Marie perched there for all of three seconds before she tipped over and fell off. The audience roared with laughter, a response that registered keenly with five-year-old Marie. Years later she recounted the incident in an interview, saying, "I got my first laugh with a fall, and I've been doing 'em ever since."

When Marie declared her independence and set out for a life unknown in the theater, her father saw there was no stopping her. He wasn't too thrilled about his daughter joining *those types*, and demanded that she change her name so as not to sully the great "Koerber" lineage. A name was a small price to pay for her freedom, reasoned Marie. She agreed, taking her middle name and borrowing the last name of a German aunt she had never met, Dressler.

Marie had the will, determination, and tenacity to succeed as an actress in traditional theater, but she lacked something that was, sadly, fundamental even in the nineteenth century: ideal features. Marie was tall and extremely stout. She had a wide, thick face, and a wonderfully expressive mouth and eyes. Some described her bluntly as "fat" and "mannish." These were not advantages—yet.

While in a touring company, Marie performed mainly in comic operas—plays imported from France and Italy with predictable plots and characters. Marie was not "beautiful peasant girl #3" material. Instead she played supporting roles that often required her to do lots of comic business, which she did—like a boss.

Tired of the touring life, Marie struck out for New York City, the mecca of theater in America then, as it is now. She hoped to land steady employment with one of the city's numerous theaters. Marie ended up drawing the attention of Maurice Barrymore, an influential playwright and actor who changed the course of her life and career with one comment: "You were born to make people laugh, Marie." Luckily for the rest of us, Marie agreed. Her looks and size were no longer liabilities—they were the secret weapons in her comic arsenal.

Barrymore cast Marie in a role in a comedy he had just written, parodying the Robin Hood story. The play tanked hard, but it was enough to get Marie noticed by critics and producers alike. Her career gained steady momentum, setting her on a path to fully embrace and seriously develop the ribald, raucous, rowdy, no-holds-barred style of comedy that few women were attempting at the time.

If there was a sofa onstage, Marie was sure to tumble over it. If there was a too-small chair, Marie inevitably became wedged in its stifling embrace. In one of her first breakout roles in the play *The Lady Slavey* (1896), Marie performed a frenzied, bombastic dance sequence with her costar, a short, slender actor named Will Daley. The first time the pair performed the dance on opening night, Daly could barely keep up with the velocity of Marie's steps, which she exaggerated for laughs. He must have looked like one of those cartoon chipmunks trying not to get crushed under the wheels of a freight train. As they started off-stage, Marie was struck by an impulse and whispered to her costar, "Jump on my hip and I'll carry you off." Daly hesitated for a split second—jump on the train or get crushed—before obliging. Thunderous applause and screeches of delight rained down in the theater. Daly never hesitated again.

As Marie's popularity grew, so did her comedic feats. In 1910 she landed the role of Tillie Blobs, a beleaguered sad-sack character in a 1910 comedy called *Tillie's Nightmare.*

people sneezing, and horses galloping. It also must have been immensely satisfying and hilarious to see Marie, in all her corpulent glory, become airborne, dangling above the stage like a great grand piano airlifted from a house.

Fortunately for Marie, her comic work translated easily to silent films, a rapidly growing entertainment in the nineteen teens. She was wooed by director Max Sennett to star opposite Charlie Chaplin in another Tillie vehicle—*Tillie's Punctured Nightmare.*

> *"We have learned to take life seriously, but never ourselves."*
>
> — MARIE DRESSLER

Over the course of the show, Marie crashes around the stage as a seasick Tillie aboard a yacht. Later on, in what must have been the play's most spectacular moments, Marie gets lifted into the clouds onto a prop airplane. This was pretty high-tech and spectacular for the time. Then again, this was also during the same period when people were losing their minds over the new "moving picture" craze that consisted of thirty- and sixty-second films showing trains speeding down tracks,

By this time, Marie was forty-four years old, which is practically a crypt keeper by entertainment standards. But Marie was just reaching her comedic prime. *Tillie's Punctured Nightmare* was a tour de force of outrageous spectacle, revolving, literally, around Marie. One review described a moment in the film: "With her pachydermous behind forever getting in the way, one thrust in the wrong direction sent several mere mortals tumbling to the ground like bowling pins."

What might have seemed humiliating and demeaning to most women, and especially to women cast as sensitive ingénues, Marie heartily and humorously embraced. Her comedy became a powerful statement about the arbitrary and, honestly, fairly stupid standards of beauty and femininity women were held to during that time and have worked to undo ever since.

Marie went on to have a successful career in film comedies well into the 1930s, even landing on the cover of *Time* magazine in 1933. Tragically her life and her laughter were cut short when Marie was diagnosed with terminal cancer in 1934.

In 1909 when audiences and critics alike began falling for this funny woman, who fiercely and fearlessly turned what made her different into what made her marvelous, Marie offered a telling remark to a reporter for the *Salt Lake Herald-Republican*: "If I can play horse for people, make them laugh, as if we all were a lot of children on a lark, why, I don't care if I don't look pretty."

After all, Marie knew only too well: Looks fade, but the power of laughter lasts forever.

KRISTEN SCHAAL

[JANUARY 24, 1978–]

Kristen Schaal looked around and surveyed her audience of pigs—no, not the misogynist type, here I mean the actual animals. Kristen grew up on a working farm not far from Boulder, Colorado, surrounded by acres of land, miles of sky, and not too many close friends or neighbors. A creative and inventive kid, left to occupy herself, Kristen made up stories and songs entertaining the closest thing she had to a captive audience: pigs, cows, and the occasional group of chickens (the worst of the bunch, clucking through her entire show). This was only the beginning of what would become an entire career based on Kristen's ability to filter life through a charmingly warped lens.

Leaving Colorado for Illinois, Kristen enrolled at Northwestern University, where she fell headfirst into the vibrant Chicago improv and comedy scene. After graduating in 2000, she moved to New York to pursue a career in comedy. Like so many other show business dreamers, Kristen waitressed to make her rent while she auditioned for film, TV, and stage roles; worked as a stand-up comic; and regularly performed improv at the People's Improv Theatre. In 2005 a blurb in *New York* magazine naming Kristen one of the "Ten Funniest New Yorkers You've Never Heard Of" helped put her on the industry map. The write-up praised Kristen for the funny characters she created onstage—beguiling, nerdy, and sharp—just like Kristen herself.

The boost from *New York* magazine propelled Kristen's career; she began traveling internationally to perform in festivals and shows, honing a kind of offbeat performance style. Her shows were unlike anything that most comedians were producing at the time. Kristen conjured up plenty of oddball characters, but she also worked in short, vignette pieces, such as tongue-in-cheek dramatic readings or re-creating schmaltzy, over-the-top marriage proposals. It was a vaudeville-influenced pastiche approach to comedy that redrew the lines of what most people expected from a comedy act. Her novel show won her the Best Alternative Comedian award in 2006 at the HBO US Comedy Arts Festival in Aspen, Colorado. "Alternative" was a fine label for the girl who test-drove her earliest material in the chicken coop.

This kind of notoriety led to Kristen's breakout role as the character Meg on the series *Flight of the Conchords*. The sitcom starred real-life comedians and musicians Bret McKenzie and Jemaine Clement as hapless musicians chasing pop-star success. Kristen's

Meg was an unhinged, creepy stalker-fan, obsessed with the duo, with a libido that runs on rocket fuel and Red Bull. In 2008, Kristen became a special commentator for *The Daily Show with Jon Stewart*, eventually taking on the role of senior women's issues correspondent; in that role, she reported on sexism in politics and wage inequality with the same kind of wacky, off-kilter irreverence that made her such a versatile stand-up and character comedian.

one episode, Hazel admits her singular desire to get famous, but reveals that she does have a backup plan for her life: "Set a house on fire, rescue everyone in it, become a hero, and appear in *Playboy*." Every twisted one-liner Kristen delivered as Hazel with absolute earnestness simply reinforced Kristen's unique and inventive comic prowess.

As Kristen has continued to rack up film and television roles—*Toy Story 3*, *Bob's Burgers*, *Last Man on Earth*, and the animated

"No one knows who the real me is, so I can be a hundred different kinds of me."
—KRISTEN SCHAAL

One of her most memorable character stints was as Hazel Wassername, the cheerfully deranged new NBC page on the show *30 Rock*. At first Kristen's Hazel seems like a genuine go-getter, eager to succeed in her career. But it quickly becomes apparent that Hazel is riddled with hilariously dark ulterior motives, such as stealing Liz Lemon's life, for starters, and stopping at nothing to get discovered on TV. Kristen's complete commitment to making Hazel's irreverence seem totally valid makes her comedy sparkle. In

series *BoJack Horseman*, for which she earned a Primetime Emmy Award nomination for her voice-over work—she has also delved into other web and print projects. In 2010, she and her husband wrote a humor book titled *The Sexy Book of Sexy Sex*. In typical quirky Kristen Schaal fashion, she admitted that she first thought of writing the book using a pseudonym because who wants to imagine Kristen doing sex "stuff," but she later realized it would be pretty tough to promote without using her real name.

Kristen makes the most of every opportunity and every stage that she's on by bringing her own slightly-left-of-center take on life and wholly embracing this tilted worldview as just as true as any other perspective. The inside of Kristen's humorously contorted mind is a funhouse that she is happy to share with the rest of us, making her one of those rare funny women who doesn't need the spotlight—she brings her own.

MARIA BAMFORD

[SEPTEMBER 3, 1970–]

Maria Bamford sounds like the name of a comic book superhero. For starters, one of those awesome "Kapow!" type graphics fits perfectly in her name—BAM!ford. But more than that, Maria seems like a kind of superhero for the way that she uses comedy and her unique, off-kilter sense of humor to fight against the dark forces of her number-one nemesis: mental illness.

Maria's stand-up routine revolves around giving audiences a transparent, bizarrely funny look inside her life living with anxiety, depression, and a form of OCD called "unwanted thoughts syndrome." Her deep valleys—time spent at inpatient psychiatric units and a lifelong struggle with binge-eating and suicidal thoughts—are where the roots of her comedy grow, blossoming into more than just laughs; what Maria Bamford does is literally comic relief.

Growing up in Duluth, Minnesota, Maria gravitated toward performing—she acted in school plays and showed a great talent for the violin. Her college years were a patchwork quilt of universities and a lot of her experiences in school were colored by bouts of depression and anxiety, making an already challenging time in any young person's life that much harder. Nevertheless, Maria found ways into artistic expression. After spending two years at Bates College in Maine, she transferred to the University of Edinburgh in Scotland for a year. Though depression followed, it was there that Maria got involved in an improv troupe called the Improverts, becoming the group's first female member. Her early foray into comedy opened up new ways for Maria to explore and express her distinctive views on life and her own experiences in a way that was both liberating and healing.

After leaving Scotland, Maria returned home to Minnesota, where she earned a BA in creative writing from the University of Minnesota. She scraped together a living in Minneapolis, busking with her violin, working at a local pizza place, and doing performance art in any spaces from coffee shops to tiny theaters she could find. Around the same time, Maria became acquainted with stand-up comic Jackie Kashian, who was performing and hosting open-mics around the city. Maria began showing up to perform. She worked her violin and music into an act already riddled with eccentricities and odd observations. As Maria discovered the humor of her own lived absurdities, that put her on the path to using comedy exclusively to engage with her mental health issues.

Maria relocated to Los Angeles, where she found steady work with minor roles in movies and television. She also landed a lot of voice-over work for shows on the Cartoon Network and PBS. However, it was onstage doing stand-up where Maria had the greatest impact. She transfixed audiences with her raw vulnerability, filtered through a stage persona of someone who simultaneously recognizes and has great compassion for her challenges.

the season for it. Late fall." Handled by anyone else, this material could become sentimental (think Nicholas Sparks does stand-up), or bitter, or simply bad. But in Maria's skilled comedic hands, her authenticity as a woman managing the best she can with a less than ideal set of circumstances takes the edge off what should be quite alarming. She gains our sympathy and understanding while diminishing the power mental illness has over her.

In addition to her successful live stand-up shows, Maria has released several comedy

"I never really thought of myself as depressed as much as paralyzed by hope."

— MARIA BAMFORD

"I couldn't work for a while," she tells audiences in one of her sets. "I took about a year and a half off because I went mental." She delivers the line in a charmingly even tone. For Maria, mental illness is simply part of her, just as race or religion is part of other people's identities. She plumbs the depths of her experiences with it in a humorous way to normalize things that are anything but. In that same set, Maria continues: "I don't know if anyone here is thinking of suicide. Don't do it. It's not

albums and a number of acclaimed specials, such as *Plan B!* (2010) and *The Special Special Special* in 2012 that Maria filmed in her living room in LA in front of her parents. And in 2016, Maria's inner worlds came spilling out onto the small screen with *Lady Dynamite*, her original comedy series developed for Netflix.

The show borrows from Maria's real life. Her character, Maria, moves back to LA after spending six months away being treated for bipolar disorder. She's home to get her life back on track with the help of her agent, Bruce. Loose plots and story arcs, along with a lot of flashback, characterized the episodes that tended to unfold a lot like Maria's overall approach to comedy—subversive, inventive, and slightly surreal. Through *Lady Dynamite*, Maria created a kind of trippy funhouse aesthetic. Humor lit the way for viewers to navigate the corridors of Maria's psyche and experience life, for a little while, from her perspective. *Lady Dynamite* ran for two seasons, garnering critical acclaim and a cult following.

Maria's comedy is unmistakable. She has a keenly honed rhythm and ninja-level ability to make her dark humor land gently and pointedly. Her extraordinary ability to take something as potentially isolating as mental illness and give it meaning and resonance for all of us, while also making us laugh, is unparalleled and the very definition of devastating fearlessness. BAM!ford. That's how it's done comedian superhero style.

FANNY BRICE

[OCTOBER 29, 1891–MAY 29, 1951]

A lot of people in their thirties and forties still have no idea what they want to be when they grow up. Fania Borach knew when she was just thirteen—it was the stage or nothing. The young Jewish tween from Brooklyn had recently entered and won an amateur night competition at Keeney's Theatre, one of the area's local entertainment hot spots. Fania sang the song "When You Know You're Not Forgotten By the Girl You Can't Forget." Not exactly Taylor Swift material, but it earned Fania the grand prize: $5, which in 1904 carried a pretty big "wow" factor. That night Fania got something more valuable than her winnings: She found her calling and decided to make entertaining her lifelong pursuit. Fania quit school and struck out to make a name for herself as a singer.

Much to Fania's dismay, this turned out to be a lot harder than she thought. The first decade of the twentieth century was a boom time for the entertainment industry. The incredible wizardry of "moving pictures," first introduced in the 1890s, led to the spread of film studios and theaters that doubled as "movie houses." There was also a lot of live stage entertainment. In addition to plays and musicals, Americans enjoyed vaudeville and burlesque shows.

Vaudeville was essentially the earliest form of "variety show." The lineup included a buffet of acts—singers and dancers, comedians, jugglers, and even animal acts—that were fast-paced and heavy on visual spectacle. Burlesque, on the other hand, was a bit different. Popularized in America in the late 1800s, burlesque was all about parody and satire. The women of burlesque played male and female roles equally. Casts lampooned well-known plays, songs, and even historical events. Burlesques sent up social customs related to class hierarchies and poked fun at feminine and masculine conventions. Another thing that made burlesque a crowd favorite were the costumes. Women performed their satirical songs and dances in outfits like tunics and skirts, showing an inordinate amount of leg or shoulder. We're talking some serious calf on display. Very PG-13.

Fania struggled to find a foothold in the vast entertainment world, finally getting traction in 1908 in a popular burlesque show titled *The Girls from Happy Land Starring Sliding Billy Watson*. From the title alone, you can tell there was a lot going on in this show, the most important of which was young Fania absolutely dazzling audiences as a gifted comedian.

As she became a fixture on the burlesque theater circuit, Fania adopted the stage name that she would go by for the rest of her life, Fanny Brice. In 1910, Fanny Brice caught the attention of the entertainment impresario Florenz Ziegfeld. Ziegfeld was the Lorne Michaels of the early 1900s. He was most widely known for creating and producing the Ziegfeld Follies. These were a series of elaborate theatrical revues that featured performers—most notably, beautiful women—outfitted in outrageous costumes, such as replicas of birds or battleships, who performed highly choreographed song-and-dance numbers. The Follies made today's Las Vegas spectaculars look as dull and boring as a bowl of oatmeal. Ziegfeld caught Fanny's burlesque performance and hired her for the Follies on the spot.

This would have been a dream come true if it were not for one little wrinkle: Fanny did not fit the shapely, blonde ingénue model of the typical stunning Ziegfeld Girl. She had wide eyes, a large nose, and a wonderfully expressive mouth that could split into an exaggerated grin or laugh, or pucker in a comical scowl; Fanny's features were marvelously elastic, the perfect palette for a comedian.

There was nothing formulaic about Fanny, including the way she approached comedy, which included using slang expressions and cultural idioms from her Jewish heritage. Racialized comedy was quite popular in the early decades of the twentieth century, which was another way of saying that America still had not quite gotten the "Racism is really, really complicated and stereotypes are not helpful" memo. Fanny embraced her cultural roots in a way that endeared her to audiences and made her stand out, even if that meant it kept her from landing leading roles in the Follies.

Ultimately, the Follies' loss was Fanny's gain. In 1911 she was let out of her contract, but she forged a creative kinship with Blanche Merrill, a woman who specialized in writing for and working with female performers. Together they capitalized on Fanny's ethnicity and her deft use of self-deprecating humor, turning both elements into some of Fanny's greatest strengths as a comedian. Out of the Follies' format, Fanny came into her own, adopting various characters for songs like "Becky's Back in the Ballet" and "The Yiddish Bride." By embracing what made Fanny most unique and engaging, she was able to eventually return to the Follies in a new capacity, as an enormously funny woman. Let the blonde girls wiggle their hips and kick their legs;

Fanny had laughs to score and she got them by the fistful.

Fanny worked steadily onstage from 1918 to 1927, appearing in Follies revues as well as in other vaudeville shows. She also recorded several records. Throughout these years, Fanny honed a distinctive style of comedy that heavily played on her features and her heritage. Despite her growing success, Fanny longed to have a place in the world of "seri-ous" or dramatic acting. She doggedly pursued film roles, but most were disappointments or total failures; she even had plastic surgery to minimize the shape and size of her pronounced nose. Though her heritage played a large role in shaping her humor, Fanny struggled with the way audiences perceived her Jewishness. Fortunately for Fanny, and the rest of us, there was little she could do to diminish her comedic gift. The sensibilities that made her refreshingly different had a way of shining through no matter how Fanny tried to curb them.

Fanny's foray into radio in the early 1930s marked a significant turning point for her comedy and career. While performing in Follies revues in 1934 and 1936, Fanny developed some of her most memorable characters, like Soul Saving Sadie, a parody of popular evangelist Aimee Semple McPherson, and Modernistic Moe, a character that lampooned both burlesque dance and Martha Graham. She performed many of them for a series of very successful radio broadcasts, opening up a whole new world of performance for Fanny. One of the characters that made it to the radio was the bratty, smugly precocious toddler Baby Snooks.

Of all of Fanny's clever satires, Baby Snooks became the one most beloved by audiences, also finally giving her the stardom she had sought throughout her performing life. *The Baby Snooks Show* became a popular weekly radio program, broadcast across the country. The character was Fanny's most playful and facile creation, one that delighted

> *"Let the world know you as you are, not as you think you should be."*
> — FANNY BRICE

listeners who tuned in to follow Snooks's silly exploits and enjoy Fanny's portrayal of a funny "little girl next door."

The Baby Snooks Show remained on the airwaves throughout the 1940s even as Fanny took a brief break from performing in 1945 to recuperate from a major heart attack. The show was put on pause in 1948 to resolve a contract dispute with Fanny over a potential move to a new entertainment medium: television. With zero interest in this television business (passing fad at best, right?), Fanny resumed her work on radio in 1949 until three years later, when she suffered a stroke and passed away.

A joyful, expansive comedian who made the nuances of parody and satire look easy, Fanny Brice unlocked her most precious, funny gifts by celebrating her natural assets. And, in doing so, she became a living example of the magic that happens when you dare to show up as your most authentic self.

ELLEN DeGENERES

[JANUARY 26, 1958–]

It takes an enormous amount of guts to be funny. Ask any funny person and she will tell you that the only thing that takes more stones than baring your soul to the public through humor is maybe jumping onto a helicopter as it pulls away from the edge of an erupting volcano while a zombie army closes in on you. And that's still a big maybe.

In 1997, Ellen DeGeneres proved that funny-brave trumps action-hero-brave when she came out as a lesbian on national television. She had worked it into the plot of her popular sitcom, *Ellen,* where her character, Ellen Morgan, blurts into the microphone at an airline ticketing counter that she's gay. Ellen's guileless, earnest awkwardness makes the scene particularly funny, but her ability to manage the criticism and outrage that followed would put her in a whole other funny-brave universe.

LGBTQ rights and the wider acceptance for all diverse communities were not in the same place as they are today (and there's still a long way to go). After that groundbreaking episode of *Ellen,* some sponsors pulled their support and at least one affiliate television station in Alabama refused to air the episode. Behind the scenes, executives for the show were unhappy with Ellen's decision to come out in this way, warning her against using her show to make a political statement. And you thought comedy was about having fun, right? She stuck to her principles and even though the show was ultimately canceled in 1998, Ellen not only won an Emmy for that particular episode, but she made television and comedy history by being the first openly gay woman to star in her own sitcom.

On her way to becoming a beloved comedy icon, Ellen, who grew up in Metairie, Louisiana, briefly studied at the University of New Orleans. She ultimately decided college was not her jam and proceeded to take on various jobs, including clerical work at a law firm and waitressing at a local TGI Fridays. Ellen had no idea that making people laugh for a living was a possibility, let alone an option for her, until she found herself at a party with friends cracking people up with her off-the-cuff observations and remarks. People encouraged her to try stand-up comedy and by the age of twenty-three she was appearing at local coffeehouses and clubs, where she was not just making friends chuckle, she was making paying strangers laugh out loud.

Ellen left her odd-job life behind and began touring nationally. She got a huge break in 1986 when a scout from *The Tonight Show*

Starring Johnny Carson caught her act and booked her for the show. She won over both the audience and Carson with her signature style, made up of quirky observational humor and charming anecdotes. Ellen seemed like the funny girl–next–door. Following her set, Carson invited her to the guest couch, which was an incredibly big deal. It was like getting the keys to a Porsche for your sixteenth birthday. She was the first female comic to get Carson's "wave" over to the couch after her very first appearance.

Ellen racked up appearances on all the popular late-night television and talk shows from *The Late Show with David Letterman* to *Larry King Live*. She enjoyed steady work touring the country and appearing at festivals as a stand-up. In 1992 ABC gave Ellen her own sitcom, titled *Ellen*. The show revolved around Ellen as the owner of a bookstore and her group of friends. It showcased Ellen's style of offbeat humor and gave audiences a different type of funny leading lady, someone who resembled an average person who was also slightly neurotic, socially awkward, and who genuinely cared about her friends and her community.

After the cancellation of Ellen's show and the mixed response to her coming out, Ellen retreated from the spotlight. A funny-brave person is strong, and might even be from another galaxy entirely, but she's not unbreakable. What followed was a series of hard years for Ellen, but ultimately helped her emerge, butterfly-style, back into the spotlight in a completely new, funny role: as host of her own daytime show.

The Ellen DeGeneres Show debuted in September 2003. Like the last number of a combination lock slipping into place, Ellen unlocked the door to a place where she could be her most legitimate, open self. On her own show, she could make the kind of comedy that brought pure happiness to audiences and break through any kind of perceived barriers that existed between people. Ellen found a place where she could show that the best thing about comedy wasn't always just getting a laugh; it was making a connection with her audience and viewers.

The show is a joyful mix of Ellen's comedy, a celebration of her love for dance, and the pleasure and humanity she brings to chatting with celebrity and noncelebrity guests alike. There is also the added bonus of watching Ellen's more mischievous side take hold with brilliantly funny pranks and practical jokes and wonky games that are not unlike the inscrutable events on Japanese game shows. By 2017, the show had racked up fifty-nine Daytime Emmy Awards and counting. Ellen has also won the People's Choice Award for Favorite Daytime TV Host fourteen times, making her the winner of more of these honors than anyone in the awards' history. The facts don't lie: People adore Ellen because she loves herself and she uses her humor to lift people up and promote a more positive outlook on life.

In Ellen's early days, she was made to feel like an outsider even in a profession that she loved, one where she had worked hard to gain the respect of her peers. But by celebrating and sharing her most true, genuine self with the world through her humor and playful approach to life and comedy, Ellen smashed through barriers of acceptance for other funny people in the LGBTQ community and made the world a bit bigger and better for all of us.

"Find out who you are and be that person."
—ELLEN DeGENERES

TRACEY ULLMAN

[DECEMBER 30, 1959–]

Tracey Ullman could see that British comedians like herself had a lot of catching up to do if they wanted to rise to the level of smart, funny humor created for decades by American women. And who better for the job than Tracey herself? Trick question.

It was 1983. Tracey was in talks with a British network to develop her own comedy TV series. The British-born comedian was well-acquainted with the work of Carol Burnett, Lucille Ball, and Lily Tomlin—strong, funny women whose character work was legendary. Tracey had noted that so many of the parts for English women comics ended up as terrible, vapid stereotypes—the empty-headed secretary or the sexed-up barmaid. Or else they were the kind of giggling, simpering girls who flanked comedian Benny Hill on *The Benny Hill Show*. Hard pass on that malarkey, thought Tracey. But the folks at the British network assumed Tracey would take on similar roles in her own show. What else was there to know about putting a funny woman on TV? Turns out that answer fell somewhere between "quite a lot" and "only everything." Tracey had not achieved her modest success up to that point by doing what was most popular and she was not about to start now.

Tracey's resolve paid off. The network struck a deal with her that allowed Tracey to hire her own writers, have script approval, and even make all costuming decisions. The result was a show called *Three of a Kind* that featured Tracey, along with fellow comedians Lenny Henry and David Copperfield (not *that* David Copperfield). It was the first comedy show of its kind to showcase an empowered, funny woman who eschewed all the lame tropes and caricatures hampering British women in comedy. Tracey's show won critical acclaim—it earned a BAFTA award for Best Light Entertainment Performance in 1984—and set her further on the path to becoming one of the world's most versatile and original comedians.

Comedy was more than just a preoccupation for Tracey; it was a matter of survival. When Tracey was six, her father passed away in front of her from a sudden heart attack. After this unthinkable tragedy, the family moved from Buckinghamshire to South West London. Her mother struggled to make ends meet and often battled with bouts of depression. Despite her mother's challenges, she retained a hearty sense of humor, instilled in Tracey and her sister, Patti. To cheer her mother up, Tracey and Patti performed silly skits and songs for her, which naturally brought out Tracey's uncanny talents for mimicry and impersonation. Drawing from the rich world of people around her—neighbors, teachers, family, celebrities—Tracey brought all manner of figures to life.

Despite her obvious talents, Tracey did not conscientiously go after a career in the performing arts. At one point she contemplated becoming a travel agent and then she took a job at a paper products distribution company. The image of Tracey Ullman plugging away at a place like Dunder Mifflin sounds like it should be the premise of one of her sketches, not, you know, like her real life. In fact, it was the drudgery of her job that caused Tracey to shake off her boredom and enter a contest called "Four in a Million," sponsored by the London Royal Court Theatre. The premise of the competition involved creating a character for an improvised play based on a series of lounge acts. Tracey came up with Beverly, a born-again Christian lounge singer. She killed it. She won a London Critics Circle Theatre Award for Most Promising New Actress and the BBC took note. Tracey's groundbreaking *Three of a Kind* was not far behind.

Tracey became a household comic name in Great Britain before she decided to branch out into American television. She joined her then-husband, producer Allan McKeown, in Los Angeles and began putting together show concepts for networks. There was a bit of trial and error for Tracey. Executives recognized her talent, but they wanted to pigeonhole her into a certain type of comedian or comic actress. James Brooks, the renowned director and creator behind *The Mary Tyler Moore Show*, received a tape of Tracey's material and instantly knew she'd be perfect for her own sketch/variety show. He could tell that Tracey existed in a category all her own. Why try to make her into something she's not? he smartly reasoned. He helped her ink a deal with FOX television and on April 5, 1987, *The Tracey Ullman Show* premiered.

Surrounded by an ensemble cast, each episode of *The Tracey Ullman Show* consisted of three sketches, one of which was some kind of musical number. Brooks wanted to put the full range of Tracey's talents on display. She opened and closed the show, appearing onstage as herself to briefly talk with the audience and answer questions, similar to the way Carol Burnett hosted her show. The show was Tracey's tour de force, allowing her to morph in and out of characters that were young, old, male, female, black, white, famous, living, and dead. By the time the show wrapped in 1990, it had won ten Emmys with Tracey taking home three.

Taking some time away from the breakneck pace of television and the overwhelming demands of her show in particular (Tracey's costuming, prosthetics, and elaborate makeup for her characters alone often physically took its toll on her), Tracey took on several film and stage projects. One of those

Vanity, and Fame" or "Tracey Takes On Sex, Romance, and Fantasy." Rather than playing a wide variety of characters, Tracey developed a roster of twenty recurring characters for the series. She has gone on to evolve this type of character-driven format over the last decade to include shows about American and British politics—*Tracey Ullman's State of the Union* and *Tracey Breaks the News*.

The rich world of characters populating Tracey's comedy playground would never

"*I've always been a misfit.*"
—TRACEY ULLMAN

was a one-woman show called *The Big Love*. However, the chance to do a special for HBO lured Tracey back to the small screen with the special *Tracey Ullman Takes on New York*. It was a variation of her sketch work, revolving around a cast of characters in interrelated scenes taking place in New York City.

Tracey won two Emmys for the special, which ultimately sparked the series, *Tracey Takes On*, where each episode covered a single topic, such as "Tracey Takes On Movies,

have come to life if Tracey had allowed other people to shape her humor and the vision of what a funny woman could do and be. She broke new ground for funny women on both continents as a performer and as an influential woman driving the comedy industry. Tracey Ullman is a shape-shifter, using humor to demonstrate the freedom that comes with coloring outside the lines and the power of employing comedy to transcend the limits of gender and femininity.

PHYLLIS DILLER

[JULY 17, 1917–AUGUST 20, 2012]

"I became a stand-up comedian because I had a sit-down husband," quipped Phyllis Diller. It was a funny one-liner that got a lot of laughs every time she told it onstage, but the reality for Phyllis was no joke.

It was the 1950s. Phyllis was the mother of six and living with her family in San Leandro, California. The Dillers were struggling on just one salary and Phyllis had to find work, but high-paying jobs were going to highly qualified men. What could Phyllis do? The answer was whatever Phyllis could find, even if that meant working as an inspector at a military air base (Phyllis Diller super-spy?). She eventually put together a string of writing jobs: first a shopping column for a local newspaper and then advertising copy for a department store in Oakland, and finally copy for radio stations in the San Francisco area. A career in stand-up comedy wasn't too far behind, but it would come about unexpectedly for Phyllis.

Growing up in Ohio, Phyllis pursued interests in writing, music, and theater. She studied classical piano at the Sherwood Conservatory of Music in Chicago and went on to Bluffton College in Ohio to pursue a career as a music teacher. In her senior year, she fell in love with and married Sherwood Diller. The couple moved to California to start a family—a very large family, as it turned out.

Phyllis struggled in her role of wife and mother. Like so many other women at the time, Phyllis found it nearly impossible to live up to the pressure cooker of domestic perfection—keeping a beautiful house, raising children who never misbehaved (eye-roll), and making sure her husband was happy and had his every need enthusiastically taken care of (eye-roll so hard it risks ocular nerve damage). Sound familiar? Women travel into space and cure diseases, but we're still made to feel like garbage if we don't know how to iron a blouse or sometimes secretly wish we could put our kids on the curb with "free" signs pinned to their shirts. The more things change, the more they stay sexist and the same, as the saying kind of goes.

Turns out, Phyllis was not alone in her frustration and unhappiness. In the course of her everyday errands to the grocery store or waiting at the Laundromat, Phyllis met countless women who shared the same dissatisfaction and loneliness. Naturally outgoing, Phyllis struck up conversations with these women and ended up sharing many of her own stories about her rocky home life, peppering her tales of domestic challenges with wry, warm, self-deprecating humor. Phyllis made them laugh; she made them feel seen and understood. Word got out about this funny, slightly kooky woman around town and before long people invited her to give humorous talks at parties and school PTA meetings. It wasn't Carnegie Hall, but you've got to start somewhere.

Phyllis's husband, whom she referred to onstage as "Fang," saw that she had talent and thought she could earn money making people laugh. He encouraged her to work on her stories and material while continuing to perform any place she could, which she did—no one brought the room down at hospitals, at women's club meetings, and in church basements like Phyllis Diller. She could see it was all leading somewhere and in 1955 that destination was the Purple Onion, a hip, popular San Francisco nightclub, known for hosting rising comedians like Bob Newhart and Lenny Bruce.

Phyllis's early set was a little like a vaudeville act. She borrowed from her training as a classical pianist to perform funny songs, interspersed with jokes and short, humorous anecdotes. It would take some time for Phyllis to develop the stage persona that helped build her fame and following. But early audiences' enthusiastic responses to this witty housewife were all the barometer she needed to let her (as well as club managers) know that she was a hit in the making. The Purple Onion extended her run and soon bookings at nightclubs and theaters all over the country followed.

By the time Phyllis began appearing on well-known talk and entertainment shows, like Jack Paar's *Tonight Show* and, later, *The Ed Sullivan Show*, Phyllis and her act were transformed. She was no longer just the woman who sang a little and told jokes; she was a stand-up comedian who put the personal experiences so familiar to so many women through the comic gristmill. With her droll demeanor, Phyllis served up zingers about marriage, motherhood, and, most significantly, herself.

Phyllis knew she needed the right look to go with her material. She lightened and styled her hair in a flamboyant, spikey kind of updo. She wore garish, shapeless gowns in all types of glittery and metallic materials. Her dresses worked as part of her performance in a couple of ways. First, her clothes helped her literally stand out onstage. Second, the cut of the dresses obscured her body, making her chest flat and her figure indiscernible. No one was distracted by her appearance or could dismiss her for being "too pretty to be funny." Instead, she made her clothes work as part of her act so that when she delivered a joke about how she was "skinny as a rail, flat as a highway" it got a bigger laugh because, to audiences at least, it seemed like the truth.

She also added another ingenious element to her act—a cigarette holder. Everyone smoked in the 1950s and '60s. Women It also drew the audience's attention back to Phyllis herself. She could pose with her hand raised up to support the holder, making sure audiences were focused on her face and what she was saying.

Phyllis was a creative genius and an utter visionary. She had to be. The downside to being one of the only women performing stand-up comedy at the time is that you're one of the only women performing stand-up

> *"I wanted to become me, totally me. The more me, the better. I instinctively knew this and was right."*
> —PHYLLIS DILLER

were often seen at fancy parties smoking through long cigarette holders with the cigarette pressed into the end. You could say it gave your race toward lung cancer a bit of class. Phyllis didn't smoke, but she knew she could put the wand to fantastic use. She had a wooden cigarette fastened to the end of a holder and brandished it so convincingly that for years people remarked in articles that they saw smoke drifting from it onstage. The holder became a way for her to punctuate her more hostile lines visually, almost like an orchestra conductor marking out beats. comedy. Phyllis didn't have another woman to mentor or support her or trade notes with her about life and work in the comedy business. She had to make comedy completely her way and maybe even set a mold that someday other woman would use to build their act. And that's exactly what Phyllis did. She persisted onward as a complete original.

Phyllis enjoyed a long, successful career in film, onstage, and on television. She was a fixture on variety and game shows throughout the 1970s and '80s; she dabbled with her own briefly broadcast sitcoms and variety shows; she gave several performances as a concert pianist in the early 1980s; she took a turn in the lead role of *Hello Dolly!* on Broadway; and she continued to perform stand-up until 2002. In 2005, Phyllis wrote a memoir, *Like a Lampshade in a Whorehouse: My Life in Comedy*, where she talked openly about the highs and lows of working in the business and her personal and professional life that always kept her motivated to move forward.

Phyllis did more than open up the field of comedy for women who followed in her footsteps, like Joan Rivers, Ellen DeGeneres, Whoopi Goldberg, and, well, just about everyone else. She gave voice to a different female perspective, one that publicly exposed the double standards, frustrations, and disappointments that come with being a woman, but that was rarely addressed through humor. Phyllis put herself on the comedy hot seat, pulling no punches about her looks, her marriage, and her shortcomings as a wife and mother. And, in doing so, she gave women permission to laugh through their own defeats and challenges, and maybe even find the courage to see them less as shortcomings and more as powerful signs of a resilience we all share.

BRAVE, BOLD, BRAZEN BADASSES

TIG NOTARO

ISSA RAE

LESLIE JONES

MAYSOON ZAYID

LENA WAITHE

RACHEL BLOOM

CAMERON ESPOSITO

APARNA NANCHERLA

NASIM PEDRAD

JESSICA WILLIAMS

WANDA SYKES

Somewhere in a small Midwestern town, a woman does her first stand-up set. She tells jokes about growing up Indian in this tiny place in the middle of nowhere. The room, made up of predominantly white blue-collar folks, swells with laughter. Something like a second heartbeat pulses inside her. She feels a power knocking at her ribs, longing for release, like a genie from a lamp.

All over the world, other funny women—Latina, Muslim, disabled, transgendered, tween—experience the same awakening. Whether they realized they belonged to the tribe of comedy twenty years ago, two years ago, or two minutes ago, these women act on that awakening, taking the leap into the unknown to chase their passion for making people laugh in whatever form that takes. They are woke—comically speaking. They boldly deploy their funny over podcasts, webisodes, Twitter feeds; in burlesque troupes; with their guitars; and in their one-woman shows. These are the women who use comedy to tell untold stories and find new ways to use their superpowers to change the world.

EXTRA EXTRAORDINAIRES: Pamela Adlon · Julie Klausner · Sasheer Zamata · Iliza Shlesinger · Marie Faustin and Sydnee Washington · Dina Hashem · Patti Harrison · Lena Einbinder · Natasha Rothwell · Francesca Martinez · Sharon Horgan · You

TIG NOTARO

[MARCH 24, 1971–]

"I t's going to get a lot worse . . . before it gets worse," Lily Tomlin once joked. In 2012, this could have been Tig Notaro's year-long mantra. In the span of six months, she had weathered a breakup with her girlfriend; nearly died from a lethal intestinal disease brought on by a bad bout with pneumonia; lost her mother after she suffered a fall; and found a lump in her breast that turned out to be breast cancer. The worst country music song ever written couldn't touch the level of catastrophe that had become Tig Notaro's reality. Her life in free fall, comedy became an unlikely safety net.

Nine days after receiving her cancer diagnosis, Tig reluctantly agreed to keep a gig at Largo, one of her favorite comedy clubs in Los Angeles. Even with a comedian's preparation and rehearsal, a stand-up set can go sideways in the blink of an eye. Tig had no idea what audiences would think of her or her set when she walked onstage and said: "Hello. Good evening. Hello. I have cancer. How are *you*?" But that's how she had decided to kick off her set, the idea coming to her only hours before when she was getting ready for the show. Just thinking of the words and the bizarre absurdity of making cancer into a conversation starter sent Tig into uncontrollable fits of laughter, which

should tell you something about the comedy of Tig Notaro—not your typical stand-up routine about jobs that suck or terrible names for fro-yo flavors.

What followed Tig's first night onstage was a raw, vulnerable, honest, and darkly funny set that not only changed Tig's life and career, it became a testament to the way that humor can transform something devastating into an opportunity to find connection and meaning.

Tig found her way into comedy after gravitating to LA with friends when she was in her early twenties. Stand-up was something that Tig had followed, enjoyed, and dreamed about trying, but not in any serious way. To her, comedians were these rarefied folks, unicorns among horses. Imagine her shock when two weeks after rolling into LA, Tig found herself making people laugh, onstage, on purpose, at her first gig at a tiny spot called Little Frida's Coffee House in West Hollywood. And that was all it took for Tig to go all-in on becoming the kind of professional funny person she never even knew she could be.

Tig steadily honed her material by frequenting open-mics nearly every night around the city. She developed a wry, deadpan delivery for her skewed, observational, anecdotal humor. Her career took off; Tig toured, she landed work on TV shows like *The Sarah Silverman Program*, appeared on late night, and in 2011 released her first stand-up album, *Good One*.

The almost cartoonish run of terrible events that piled up on Tig was a catalyst for her personally and professionally. Without planning on it, the night of her Largo show, Tig took one giant step out of her comedy

hours, the album sold six thousand copies and was later nominated for a Grammy. It was an unintended windfall for Tig, brought about through horrible circumstances that, let's face it, anyone could have done without. The response to *Live* was really a connection with the honest, available self that Tig put onstage that night. Not knowing how much or how little she had to lose, Tig risked it all anyway.

"I'm the luckiest unlucky person."
—TIG NOTARO

comfort zone, away from the tone and style that had characterized her typical stand-up sets. Tig showed up onstage as a comedian, but also as a real person facing very real challenges. She invited the three hundred people in the audience to walk with her through a situation riddled with terrifying uncertainty and laugh about it anyway. The next day, Tig woke up to an inbox overflowing with messages from friends, family, fans, and the industry. *Rolling Stone* wanted to interview her; publishers wanted to sign her for a book deal.

As it turned out, Tig's Largo show had been recorded and was eventually released as her second comedy album, *Live*. Within

Tig brought more of her personal journey into comedy and her life-altering year into her memoir *I'm Just a Person* (2015) and into the 2016 documentary, *Tig Notaro: Boyish Girl Interrupted*, which became a comedy album also nominated for a Grammy. Tig also developed the semi-autobiographical scripted series, *One Mississippi*, that ran for two seasons. In 2018 it was announced that Tig had signed on to star in *First Ladies*, a Netflix comedy with Jennifer Aniston, where Aniston plays America's first woman president and Tig plays her wife, making Tig the kind of comedy badass who proves that literally anything is possible.

ISSA RAE

[JANUARY 12, 1985–]

ssa Rae elevates awkward to an awesomely funny art form. Her groundbreaking series that first debuted on the web, *The Misadventures of Awkward Black Girl*, centers on the character J, played by Issa, who works at a call center for a weight loss pill company. J maneuvers through a minefield of explosives in the form of the uncomfortable, disquieting, anxiety-provoking happenings between coworkers and friends that make up our everyday lives. Add to this Issa's salient outlook on

friend and fellow Stanford alum, Tracy Oliver (who would later work with Issa to create *Awkward Black Girl*). The two friends also took classes at the New York Film Academy. During Issa's time in New York, where she was grinding through her film and acting studies, working part-time jobs, and managing the challenges of meeting new people in a big city, she got the inspiration for *ABG*. Where there is hardship, humor is never far behind.

Mining her cringey and off-putting social

> *"I thrive on obstacles. If I'm told that it can't be done, then I push harder."*
>
> —ISSA RAE

the role race places in shaping our personal and social awkwardness and the result is comedy gold that reimagines a new world of possibilities for funny, diverse women.

Issa became interested in acting while at Stanford University. Though she was an African Studies and African-American Studies major, Issa dabbled in writing plays and making videos. She even created a mock reality series, called *Dorm Diaries*. Issa won a fellowship to the prestigious Public Theater in New York and moved to the city with her best

encounters, Issa dug into the grassroots nature of producing *ABG*. She enlisted the help of friends to act in, film, and edit the episodes, posting them on YouTube. The series found its fans and went viral, attracting media attention. Using this groundswell of support, Issa launched a successful Kickstarter campaign to fund the rest of the series. Rapper Pharrell Williams became a fan of the show and put it on his YouTube channel, which gave Issa the support she needed to continue the series and get more visibility as a creative.

Awkward Black Girl also became the title of Issa's 2015 memoir. Her frank, funny discussions about feeling like an outcast in her own skin won her a legion of admirers and propelled the book to become a *New York Times* best seller.

In 2013 Issa teamed up with Larry Wilmore to develop a comedy pilot with her as its star. It would take four years, tons of hard work, and more than a little bit of faith, but Issa eventually brought her HBO sitcom, *Insecure,* to life. *Insecure* focuses on the friendship between Issa (played by Issa) and Molly (played by Yvonne Orji), who are best friends in their twenties, experiencing life after college in South Los Angeles. Jobs, relationships, the hustle of city living, and, most of all, the realities of being black women in this current moment, all become funny, poignant fodder for the women living their best "insecure" lives.

Insecure earned Issa two Golden Globe nominations with more to surely follow as it enters into its next season and beyond. Issa has done more than craft an intelligent, witty show that offers original takes on black culture and black female friendships. She has helped to orchestrate a shift in the comedy and show business industries toward executive support for shows featuring diverse characters and writers.

Onscreen, Issa can keep serving up her awkward humor rooted in the insecurities that so many of us recognize, and we'll keep reaping the benefits of her uncomfortable laughter. But behind the scenes for this comedy power player, it's clearly nothing but confidence.

LESLIE JONES

[SEPTEMBER 7, 1967–]

At one point, Leslie Jones thought she might be a lawyer. No offense, justice system, but we're glad that never panned out. However, it isn't hard to imagine the hilariously honest, outspoken comedian standing in a courtroom giving the judge and jury a piece of her brilliantly funny mind. (Network Execs of the World, if you're reading this: I would totally watch that show.) After all, this was the same woman whose uninhibited Twitter enthusiasm for the 2018 Winter Olympic Games got her a network spot as a commentator from South Korea. Leslie is the most awesome kind of runaway train type of funny.

Leslie always loved comedy. She grew up watching performers like Richard Pryor, Carol Burnett, and Whoopi Goldberg, but never thought comedy was something she could do or make a career out of. A basketball scholarship earned Leslie a place at Colorado State University, where she became a DJ for the campus radio station and won a contest for the "Funniest Person on Campus." A friend signed Leslie up for the contest without her knowing; we all have that certain person we can count on to shove us into one humiliating situation after the next, right? But Leslie's friend knew what she was doing; she thought Leslie was one of the funniest women on campus and everyone, especially Leslie, deserved to know it. Get onstage, start talking, and be yourself, she told a skeptical Leslie; the rest will sort itself out. Miraculously, it did. Leslie won the contest. Apparently, this comedy stuff might be something she could actually do. Leslie withdrew from school, packed up, and moved to Los Angeles to start her comedy career in earnest.

Leslie worked the stand-up clubs in LA and in 2008 she was hired to tour with comic Katt Williams on his *It's Pimpin' Pimpin'* tour. This took Leslie on a massive circuit, playing to crowds in 107 cities in six months. It was grueling, but rewarding. From the material she worked on while on tour, she filmed a Showtime comedy special titled *Problem Child*. Leslie was becoming known as an exciting new face on the stand-up circuit, who brought a straightforward, tell-it-like-it-is swagger to her jokes and funny stories. She also had the added gift of an expressive physical presence—Leslie slayed audiences as she punctuated her jokes and bits with exaggerated facial expressions. Leslie's strong, uninhibited performance style offered a fresh contribution to the stand-up stages, filling clubs and theaters with contagious energy.

Onstage, she relished taking risks and making up her own set of rules as she went along.

Leslie hauled herself up the comedy ladder rung by rung until she hit a ceiling that sent her tumbling down back to square one: Opening one night for Jamie Foxx, Leslie completely bombed and was booed off the stage. Leslie was shattered worse than a jilted girlfriend in a Taylor Swift song. Later Foxx took her out for a bite of food, sympathy, and tough love, telling her that she had enormous

auditioning for a performing role. A year after working behind the scenes, she was bumped up to being a featured player. Her addition to the cast was the first time in the show's history that more than one African-American woman was represented on the show at one time. The world was about to get a lot more of Leslie Jones and that was not remotely a bad thing.

When she wasn't bringing down the house with her impersonations of Condo-

"I just like to bring the funny."
—LESLIE JONES

talent, but no life experience. She was still young and just out of college and hadn't really lived. Leslie took Foxx's perspective to heart. She left professional comedy in the rearview for six years while she held all kinds of jobs— cook, waitress, cashier—and got around to, as Foxx said, really living life.

When she returned to the comedy scene in 2013 she had a broader worldview to draw from and was ready to unleash the full range of her facile mind on the world. She even found a new way to grow her comedy: writing. Leslie joined the *SNL* writing staff after

leeza Rice, Michelle Obama, or Donna Brazile, Leslie was a frequent guest at the Weekend Update desk. Whether commenting on things like a newfound love for baseball or her surprising discovery that an African-American invented the traffic light—"Maybe I would have respected the traffic light a little more if I knew it was a signal coming from a brother!"—Leslie brought an infectious zeal for comedy. It shone through in every sketch, no matter what the topic or scenario: Leslie owned the scene just by being 1,000 percent unapologetically Leslie Jones.

That energy and persona translated easily to the big screen. In 2016 Leslie joined the cast of director Paul Feig's *Ghostbusters*. Leslie played MTA worker–turned–Ghostbuster team member Patty Tolan, alongside comedy powerhouses Kate McKinnon, Kristen Wiig, and Melissa McCarthy. The movie sparked some skepticism (a nice way of saying "extreme anger") from various fans and critics that this ensemble of women could take the Ghostbusters franchise into the twenty-first century. Leslie's rapid-fire quips and comebacks, delivered with her signature comic fortitude, put a lot of that doubt to rest, making for some of the movie's funniest and most memorable scenes.

Raw comic energy that cannot be contained might be the best way to describe the powerhouse that is Leslie. The girl who once thought she was destined to become the next Eddie Murphy has become something even better: the one and only Leslie Jones.

MAYSOON ZAYID

[SEPTEMBER 7, 1974–]

Stop me if you've heard this one before: A female Muslim comedian with cerebral palsy scores a gig doing a comedy set for the 2016 Republican National Convention. Not. A. Joke. This is the bonkers, amazing, incredible life of Maysoon Zayid, your not-so-average Palestinian funny girl next door.

Maysoon grew up in New Jersey, dreaming of an acting career. She attended the University of Arizona, where she studied drama and performance. After college, Maysoon landed minor roles on the soap opera *As the World Turns* and the police drama *Law and Order*.

Shocking to no one who has spent more than ten minutes in show business, Maysoon was met with resistance from casting directors who couldn't see past her disability or ethnicity to give her a chance. Rather than shelve her dream, Maysoon simply drew up a new one: comedy. Maysoon identified with funny women who had come before her, such as Whoopi Goldberg and Rosie O'Donnell. They didn't quite fit industry standards of ideal cultural or physical types, so they turned their differences into comedy gifts and connected with people across race and religion with their humor. A similar kind of attitude gave Maysoon the confidence to explore and relay her own personal, cultural experiences with material that is smart, disarming, and very funny.

Maysoon began performing in well-known clubs throughout New York, including Caroline's and Gotham. In 2003 she cofounded the New York Arab-American Comedy Festival with fellow comic Dean Obeidallah and debuted her own one-woman show, *Little American Whore*, directed by comedian Kathy Najimy at Los Angeles's Comedy Central Stage.

Her 2014 TED talk, "I've Got 99 Problems and Palsy Is Just One," brought her sharp, pointed humor to a global audience. In her presentation, Maysoon covers a lot of cultural and comedy commentary—xenophobia, stereotypes regarding disability, feminism,

> *"And if I can, you can."*
> — MAYSOON ZAYID

religion, and terrorism. She builds a bridge of jokes between herself—a disabled Muslim woman—and the audience, proving that laughter can be a powerful key to understanding, compassion, and change.

In the midst of her busy schedule, Maysoon dedicates three months out of every year to travel to the Palestinian Territories, where she runs workshops for disabled and orphan children in refugee camps. Using humor, art, and creativity, Maysoon helps these children process and work through their grief and trauma.

And as far as that RNC show? Maysoon killed it. She may have ninety-nine problems, but comedy isn't one of them.

LENA WAITHE

[MAY 17, 1984–]

A lot of parents think watching too much television is unhealthy for their kids. They don't want them to become lazy or antisocial or Emmy Award–winning comedy writers, right? Wait, what? Thanks to TV, by the age of seven, future Emmy Award winner Lena Waithe knew she wanted to be a television writer.

Lena grew up on the South Side of Chicago. She was raised by her single mother, who worked full time to support her family, and her grandmother. Television was a constant companion for the threesome, but especially for Lena and her grandmother, who watched hours of programming together when Lena came home from school. On the screen, Lena saw African-Americans both like herself and not like herself on shows such as *A Different World*, *The Cosby Show*, *The Jeffersons*, and *Good Times*. These representations would create powerful imprints on Lena's consciousness, which would affect her creative life later on. Lena was also an avid reader and writer. She was wired for storytelling from childhood, but could never have known that some day her own funny, moving stories about life on Chicago's South Side, about being a young, black, gay woman searching for the right way to come out to her mother, would earn her a place in television, comedy, and cultural history.

Lena followed her creative interests to Columbia College in Chicago, where she earned a degree in Cinema and Television Arts. Then she moved to LA and found steady gigs writing for FOX and Nickelodeon, while simultaneously working on various film and web projects. In 2015, she was invited to a meeting with comedian Aziz Ansari, who was casting for a new comedy series titled *Master of None*. The pair immediately clicked and Lena was offered the part of Denise, Ansari's best friend. The part had originally been written for a straight white woman, but everyone on the show's staff loved Lena's strong, funny demeanor and appreciated the viewpoint she brought to dating and relationships as a gay woman.

On the show, Denise sees her best friend, Dev (played by Ansari), through heartache and dating missteps, all the while keeping it real; she supports him and calls him out on his issues and juvenile nonsense, just as any true best friend would. This is one of the things that makes Lena's portrayal of Denise unique: She's genuine and three-dimensional and she's not there to be a punch line about sexuality or race. Lena grounds Denise through her self-possession, her vulnerability, and her humor.

The episode titled "Thanksgiving" centers on Denise and traces her journey to coming out as a young, gay woman first to Dev (on Thanksgiving) and then to her mother (on a subsequent Thanksgiving). Through flashbacks, viewers see the full range of Denise's path from accepting herself to navigating the rocky terrain of gaining acceptance from create, write, and star in *The Chi*, a scripted drama that explores the lives and experiences of families living on Chicago's South Side. It's gritty and poignant and punctuated with Lena's singular brand of understated humor.

Lena's work in front of the camera already puts her in an entirely new stratosphere of smart, funny women, but her efforts behind the scenes and within the

> *"The things that make us different, these are our superpowers."*
> —LENA WAITHE

the rest of her family. Cowritten by Lena and Ansari, "Thanksgiving" mirrors Lena's real-life experience coming out to her family. She elegantly tempers the emotional intensity of the script with plenty of humor, making it one of the show's most unforgettable and moving episodes. A lot of people felt the same way, and in 2017, Lena became the first African-American woman to win an Emmy for Outstanding Writing for a Comedy Series.

Since wrapping her second season on *Master of None*, Lena has shifted gears to industry make her a mighty change agent. Whether as a creative, propelling her own projects, or helping to open up new opportunities for other women, Lena fights hard to make inclusivity and acceptance of diversity one of her driving missions working in the business. She knows that somewhere there's a little girl parked in front of a TV or clutching an iPad, watching shows about people and families who look like her. Lena knows what that spark of recognition could ignite and she is not about to disappoint.

RACHEL BLOOM

[APRIL 3, 1987–]

Take one musical theater nerd, one legendary sci-fi author, and a ton of guts, and what you get is Rachel Bloom's 2010 twisted musical comedy video love letter, "F— Me, Ray Bradbury." In it, Rachel channels her inner Britney Spears in pigtails and outfitted in a Catholic school–style skirt and blouse, belting out her love, longing, and insatiable lust for the ninety-year-old literary genius behind *Fahrenheit 451* and *The Martian Chronicles*. "F— Me, Ray Bradbury" is a smart, wickedly funny musical parody that is not even the most inventive thing to spring from Rachel's brain; it was simply the first that introduced the masses to her brand of sharp, salacious satire.

Rachel came out of NYU's prestigious Tisch School of the Arts with a degree in drama, majoring in musical theater. While at NYU, Rachel became particularly interested in sketch comedy. She served as the head writer and director of the campus sketch group, Hammerkatz, and after graduation stayed in New York to take classes and perform at Upright Citizens Brigade (UCB).

In the midst of performing improv, sketch, and even stand-up, Rachel began working on various music video projects. One of these ultimately became her infamous Valentine to her favorite sci-fi author. She launched the video on YouTube in 2010 to coincide with the writer's ninetieth birthday. Some people get gift cards or flowers. Not so for Ray Bradbury. Rachel's comedy homage went viral, establishing her as a keen, funny humorist, taking on musical comedy in an entirely fresh, new way.

Two comedy music albums followed before Rachel successfully landed a deal with the CW network for her idea for a scripted show that was both a sitcom and a musical comedy. In 2015 audiences stepped into the lovably neurotic, vaguely unsettling, incredibly inventive musical world of *Crazy Ex-Girlfriend*.

As its writer and star, Rachel helms a comedy tour de force with *Crazy Ex-Girlfriend*. The show follows the disastrous misadventures of Rebecca Bunch, played by Rachel, as she impulsively uproots her life as a successful lawyer in New York to move to California in an effort to reconnect with (read: befriend and stalk) a boyfriend from her teen years. Each episode features elaborate musical numbers borrowing from every kind of musical performance genre imaginable—theater, music videos, film musicals—featuring Rachel's unmistakable, perverse comic sensibility.

Given the show's premise, there's a lot

that could go off the rails to make it feel like a predictable stereotypical romcom, trimmed down for television. However, Rachel injects *Crazy Ex* with sophisticated humor and a lot of feminist nuance. Complicated, dynamic female friendships are at the heart of the show. Power dynamics in the office and in the bedroom tilt toward women. And amid the funny song-parody scenes with their highly choreographed dances, the show wades into some emotionally intense territory with story lines around abortion, mental illness, and depression.

So what's next for Rachel? Wherever her deliciously contorted comedy brain takes her and us next.

> "When you wrap up your self-worth with your talent, and suddenly you might not be the most talented, that's really scary. And I think that fear is in part why I turned to comedy because I had no expectations of being a comedian. It was exciting to get good at something where I wasn't afraid of not being the best."
>
> —RACHEL BLOOM

CAMERON ESPOSITO

[OCTOBER 17, 1981–]

Cameron Esposito has never met a boundary she didn't mind breaking or, at the very least, seriously denting. Take for instance her 2018 comedy special, *Rape Jokes a* one-hour stand-up set she first debuted in clubs throughout the country. *Rape Jokes* is a brave, innovative way to use the power of comedy to heal trauma while encouraging dialogue. She explores the nuances of sexual violence with humor, compassion, poignancy, and carefully crafted rage in observations and anecdotes that lead up to Cameron recounting her own experience with sexual assault.

In the era of #MeToo, which has brought untold exposure to the climate of assault and harassment permeating every part of our lives and culture, including the comedy scene, Cameron has staked a claim to a space for survivors and their stories. Humor is Cameron's conduit to healing, dialogue, and change. Eager to take her hour-long set to the masses, Cameron filmed *Rape Jokes* as a special and put it online with a "pay what you can" structure, with a portion of the proceeds benefitting sexual assault advocacy organizations. It's comedy with a cause and marks only one in a run of milestones for Cameron that have shaped her career and made her one of the most impactful funny women today.

After graduating from Boston College with a degree in theology and English, Cameron set her sights on returning to her native Illinois to become a social worker. This nearly panned out except for one small issue: at Boston College Cameron had joined the improv troup, My Mother's Fleabag, and she discovered that making people laugh onstage was better than finding a money tree in your backyard. Cameron moved to Chicago and began taking courses in social work at the University of Chicago only to find that this whole cracking up audiences thing was not a phase. She left school and decided to give stand-up comedy a try.

She quickly immersed herself in the Chicago comedy scene, performing both improv and stand-up, becoming a staple performer at the popular Lincoln Lodge. Cameron found the stand-up scene for women to be thin at best, and for queer women, practically nonexistent. She paved the way for all kinds of funny women not only by showing up at clubs and open-mics with a Rocky-type relentlessness, but by developing "The Feminine Comique," a stand-up comedy class at the Lincoln Lodge just for women. The classes took off, and soon Cameron found herself not just teaching traditional comic hopefuls, but all kinds of women—collection officers and marketing executives—interested in unlocking the benefits of bringing a little more laughter into their lives. Cameron's rules were pretty simple: no cat jokes, no self-deprecating humor, and own your sense of humor proudly.

slim, side-mulleted Ms. Esposito. Surmising that Butcher was there for more than the cheap beer and greasy food, Cameron asked, "So when are you going to go up?" Always the consummate supporter of fellow funny women, Cameron got more than she bargained for from that first conversation. She and Butcher would go on to date, marry, and

"My personal philosophy is talk about whatever you want on a show, but it better be good. And especially if it's something that challenges folks. You don't want to be on the side of power to demean a group that is at risk. Because that's propaganda. Whenever you're on the side of power, you're not making art. Art upends power."

— CAMERON ESPOSITO

Women could be funny and powerful by tapping into their unique, awesome selves. Weak sauce stereotypes need not apply.

While steadily developing her material and performing regularly throughout the Midwest, Cameron met Rhea Butcher, another hopeful stand-up. Butcher frequented a bar not far from her house where Cameron routinely performed. One night, Butcher found herself having a conversation with the tall,

even star in their own scripted comedy, *Take My Wife*. The show was loosely based on Cameron and Butcher's life, featured a staff of all women writers, and won the two comics high critical praise for the way it brought a fresh, authentic perspective to the sweet, funny, and challenging nuances of a same-sex relationship. In 2018, Cameron and Butcher separated to take personal time apart and work on their respective careers.

Cameron has become a familiar presence across all kinds of media—film, television, podcasts, and sites like BuzzFeed and YouTube. She made her first appearance on late night in 2013 with a set on *The Late, Late Show with Craig Ferguson,* the same night Jay Leno was on as a guest. Cameron took a funny, soft shot at people's obsession with denim, aiming it squarely at Leno, infamous for his denim-centric wardrobe. She has released five comedy albums and hosts the popular smart, witty podcasts *Put Your Hands Together* and *Queery*. The latter podcast has Cameron sitting down for thoughtful, probing, always humorous conversations with other icons in the LGBTQ community. *Queery* is part of Cameron's larger mission to deploy comedy to educate and enlighten as much as it is to entertain. She brings this to bear in another ongoing project, the "Ask a Lesbian" video series where she tackles all the pressing questions related to her sexuality, including: "Do you find Ellen attractive?," "Is it easier for you to be a stripper?," and "Can you help me install my heater?" Cameron fields both slightly silly and more serious questions (ones, for example, relating to same-sex marriage rights or coming out to one's family) with her characteristic levity, but also with great compassion and earnestness.

After all, truth matters to Cameron, in her personal and professional life. Her sexuality, as well as the politics and culture of the LGBTQ community and its history, play a large role in her projects, whether that's stand-up sets, TV or film scripts, podcasts, essays, or guest appearances. Cameron represents the challenges and joys of being a gay woman without resorting to lazy stereotypes or making people feel uncomfortable for the sake of being provocative or edgy. Her successes serve as important statements about the need for inclusivity in the expanding comedy universe. She makes humor her not-so-secret weapon as she uses comedy to inform and, above all, make people laugh about the commonalities that knit us together and the differences that deserve celebrating.

APARNA NANCHERLA

[AUGUST 22, 1982–]

How do you make a hilarious podcast about depression? You put it in the hands of professional funny woman and "certified depressive" Aparna Nancherla. Aparna hosts the *Blue Woman Group* podcast, along with fellow comedian Jacqueline Novak, where the two talk openly and humorously about depression and anxiety. They dig into topics that range from surviving the Thunderdome of social media to pushing past the shame of crying at work. Aparna and Novak world where you often feel like you're trying to climb up a never-ending escalator moving downward. Both in her stand-up and on *Blue Woman Group*, Aparna puts a sardonic, silly spin on depression and anxiety, confidently owning her weirdness so that you can own yours, too.

Skilled in both improv and stand-up comedy, Aparna tended to be the one in her group of friends ready with a sarcastic comment or a funny, offbeat take on a person or situation.

> *"Do what you think is funny, not what the audience thinks is funny."*
> —APARNA NANCHERLA

treat everything up for discussion with levity, compassion, and depth. Ultimately, they're making fun of pretty serious issues that, ironically, requires a certain amount of seriousness. It's like a comedy chicken-and-egg situation. But, most importantly, it works.

Aparna has dealt with depression her entire life. It's an especially tricky situation for Aparna, who is Indian and hails from a culture where mental illness is heavily stigmatized and shrouded in silence. Humor has become the way Aparna makes sense of a But Aparna never thought she'd end up with a career as a comedian. On her twentieth birthday, she decided to see if there was anything to her natural wit by performing her first stand-up set. Most people settle for a nice dinner and some gifts; Aparna decided to risk total public humiliation by telling jokes to a roomful of strangers. The risk paid off. She was on her way.

After graduating from Amherst College with a degree in psychology, Aparna moved back home to Washington, DC, and began performing and studying comedy. She trained at the Washington Improv Theater and did sets at clubs around the city. A move to LA brought her one of her first major TV opportunities, writing for *Totally Biased with W. Kamau Bell.*

On *Totally Biased*, Aparna got to develop and perform her own material on camera. It helped her become more comfortable onscreen and it also gave her a space to expand on the kind of comedy she brought to her stand-up—irreverent perspectives on life and her own experiences, tinged with a slightly dark undertone.

After leaving *Biased*, Aparna wrote for *Late Night with Seth Meyers* before deciding to focus on developing her own projects. She released her first comedy album, *Just Putting It Out There*, in 2016 and also appeared on Comedy Central's *Half Hour* stand-up series. Most recently, Aparna wrapped a stint as a series regular on the sitcom, *Corporate*—a comedy centering around two employees working for a generic soul-sucking corporation. Misery loves comedy, as the saying actually should go.

Whether writing, performing stand-up, podcasting, or effortlessly filling Twitter feeds with her desert-level, dry humor—"Team apathy for the whatever" and "I like to call therapy baggage claim"—Aparna defuses the struggles that so many of us share with equal parts wit and novelty and a whole bucket of brave.

NASIM PEDRAD

[NOVEMBER 18, 1981–]

It's every comedian's nightmare; well, after the one about bombing in front of a stadium of people that includes all your comedy heroes living and dead. It's the nightmare about coming face-to-face with someone in real life that you make fun of for a living. This was Nasim Pedrad's waking horror. For five seasons on *Saturday Night Live*, Nasim stole sketch after sketch parodying the infamous reality TV star, Kim Kardashian. Nasim killed it in sketches like "Waking Up with Kimye" —a morning talk show hosted by Kim and her husband, Kanye West—or while she was working the Weekend Update desk to dish about her sister Khloe's wedding. Nasim gave audiences a pitch-perfect incarnation of Kim, complete with a nasal drawl and vacant, languid stare into space at nothing in particular.

Then one night at an industry event Nasim bumped into Kim. A vortex of panic worse than showing up for a job interview with spinach stuck in your teeth and a giant, throbbing zit on the end of your nose engulfed Nasim. The reality TV star approached the comedian. Nasim tensed, waiting for the yelling, maybe even some drink-tossing. "Do we really sound like that?" Kim innocently asked with a smile, referring to the high, nasal whine of Nasim's Kim voice. She was perfectly pleas-

ant and for Nasim that became one of her most affirming moments as a comedian: She had done her job so well that even the person at the center of her impression bought it.

Nasim landed at *SNL* in 2009 as the show's first female Middle Eastern cast member. Born in Tehran, Iran, Nasim and her family emigrated to the United States when she was a young child, settling in Irvine, California. As a kid, *SNL* became an important part of Nasim's life long before she would find herself in front of its live studio audience. Watching the show helped Nasim assimilate into her new country, learning about America's culture, trends, and sense of humor.

Nasim was a dedicated theater geek in junior high and high school, eventually going on to study drama at UCLA. Though she was exposed to a huge range of theater in college, Nasim found herself gravitating toward comic roles. After graduation, she stayed in LA, where she enrolled at the Groundlings and became a member of the prestigious Sunday Company. During her stint at the Groundlings, Nasim developed a one-woman show titled *Me, Myself & Iran*. In the show, she portrayed five distinct Iranian characters, exploring the culture and perspectives through these distinct figures.

The show became a way for Nasim to demonstrate her comic range as well as to perform characters that most audiences, especially American audiences, were not used to seeing, at least not with any kind of depth or dimension. *Me, Myself & Iran* was Nasim's *siasm*, and *Brooklyn Nine Nine*. In 2017 it was announced that Nasim would be part of Disney's live-action *Aladdin* reboot, playing the part of Dalia, Jasmine's best friend. In Nasim's hands, the new character promises to add both comic relief and plenty of oppor-

> *"I knew at a young age that I wanted to do comedy, and maybe part of that was trying to fit in at school because I had a weird name, and my parents had these accents, and I was definitely a late bloomer."*
>
> —NASIM PEDRAD

way of using comedy to challenge and break down cultural barriers. It also got the attention of Tina Fey who saw one of Nasim's performances and recommended she audition for *SNL*, which in the comedy world is a lot like getting a phone call from Oprah.

Since leaving *SNL*, Nasim has gone on to appear in several sitcoms, including *Mulaney, New Girl, Scream Queens, Curb Your Enthu-* tunities to make sly, funny jabs at things that transcend cultural differences, such as friendship, relationships, and, of course, how to redecorate the inside of a lamp with vintage finds. In fact, Nasim seems to possess a genie-like versatility of her own, conjuring up characters as diverse as Arianna Huffington and Aziz Ansari with dizzying ease and her own special brand of bold, funny magic.

JESSICA WILLIAMS

[JULY 31, 1989–]

Like a lot of college seniors, Jessica Williams found herself studying for her finals at Cal State Long Beach while also prepping for a new job in New York City. However, unlike her classmates heading off to jobs at accounting firms or cool tech start-ups, Jessica's gig was a little bit different. Okay, it was *a lot* different. She was about to join the cast of *The Daily Show with Jon Stewart* as the show's first African-American female correspondent. No pressure. Not in the least bit distracting. What overdue astronomy lab?

Even as a teenager, Jessica flourished in the performing arts scene. A Los Angeles native, Jessica attended Nathaniel Narbonne High School and became heavily involved in the school's theater program. She got her first laugh performing with her school's improv team as a freshman and knew that comedy was where she belonged.

After high school, Jessica struck a balance between taking college classes and going out for auditions for film and television. In 2006 her hard work paid off and she landed a starring role in the short-lived Nickelodeon sitcom *Just for Kicks*. Unfortunately, *Just for Kicks* was not going to make Jessica's comedy career. After the show was canceled, Jessica returned to her life as a student/actor. She continued going out for roles, working on her college degree, and also began taking classes and performing at Upright Citizens Brigade (UCB) in LA, an experience that helped her develop and refine her comic sensibilities.

Six years later, Jessica learned that *The Daily Show* was hiring. Anyone seriously into the comedy scene as a fan or a performer had followed *The Daily Show* as it evolved from a satirical news program to a cutting-edge comedy and news show, pulling zero punches about everything from politics and sexism to racism and poverty. At the urging of a casting director, Jessica submitted a tape. She was sure they would toss her reel in the "Good God NO!" pile (a real thing, apparently). Her anxiety made sense. After all, auditioning for a major television show that could change the course of your entire life is no small thing.

Turned out, Jessica's worry was unfounded; Jon Stewart himself called Jessica to invite her to fly to New York for a formal audition. In January 2012, twenty-two-year-old Jessica Williams punched in at her first day on the job at as *The Daily Show's* senior youth correspondent.

The Daily Show not only gave Jessica a crash course in comedy, but also one in politics and current events. The fast-moving stream of what often feels like a thirty-two-hour daily news cycle means that writers and cast members on any of these types of shows have to work quickly to synthesize events and create stories or segment pitches. Jessica dove in feetfirst as she wrote and broadcast field reports and other news segments, providing a fresh take as both a young person and an African-American woman. It allowed Jessica to speak up about issues like inequality and rac-

she addresses the Wall Street "thugs" in question, saying, "If you don't want to be associated with white-collar crime, maybe you shouldn't dress that way!" Clearly, a funny and fearless new comic journalist was on the scene, changing the show's comic chemistry in a very real way.

While working on *The Daily Show*, Jessica became friends with another fantastic, funny woman named Phoebe Robinson. Robinson

"It's impossible to be perfect and you won't do a good job if you're too focused on proving yourself to others."
—JESSICA WILLIAMS

ism in a way that was both bitingly funny and critically insightful. For instance, Jessica tackled New York City's controversial "stop and frisk" law for one of her field reports. Broadcasting from Wall Street—in Jessica's words, "one of the city's most notorious, crime-ridden neighborhoods"—she blasts the law's inherent racism. She comically urges the police to do something about the white-collar criminals flooding the neighborhood. She takes a satirical jab at our racial and cultural biases when

was a stand-up comic who did background research for the show. As the two became friends, Jessica casually mentioned that she'd always wanted to try stand-up. And as friends tend to do for one another, Robinson gave Jessica the push she needed to make it happen for real. Robinson invited Jessica to cohost her monthly live comedy show, *Blaria LIVE!* Based on Robinson's popular blog, the show featured a showcase of stand-up and special guests, hosted by Robinson and performed at UCB.

Jessica had a blast on her first *Blaria LIVE!*, discovering that she and Robinson had an easy, natural comedy chemistry. They began to work on the show together, developing a rapport that featured Jessica and Robinson exchanging witty, candid observations about everything from sex and race to relationships, families, and jobs. The live performance morphed into a podcast titled *2 Dope Queens*, which launched in April 2016, and quickly became one of iTunes's most downloaded podcasts. The podcast retained the same format as the live show, with Jessica and Robinson, along with a diverse lineup of comedians of all different cultural and gender identities. The success of *2 Dope Queens* put Jessica and Robinson on the map as one of the funniest, most original comedy duos. They became such fan favorites that HBO inked a deal with the duo to produce four hour-long *2 Dope Queen* specials in 2018.

After Jessica parted ways with *The Daily Show* in 2016, she put the pedal down on all things comedy. In addition to working closely with Robinson on the podcast and live shows of *2 Dope Queens*, Jessica starred in the 2017 not-your-average-romcom flick, *The Incredible Jessica James*. The movie finds Jessica playing an aspiring playwright who falls for a divorced app developer played by Chris O'Dowd. *The Incredible Jessica James* was written by Jim Strouse *for* Jessica. No pressure, more like just another day in the life of one very funny, dope queen.

WANDA SYKES

[MARCH 7, 1964–]

There is absolutely nothing funny about the National Security Administration. That's what Wanda Sykes realized when she worked there as a procurement officer in 1987. Wanda joined the NSA out of college, equipped with a marketing degree from Hampton University. It was Wanda's job at the NSA to find the best deals for their various products and services. If reading that last sentence caused you to nod off, think how Wanda felt: Here was a woman who made people around the office laugh with her conversational wit, spending eight hours a day on the phone haggling over the price of software and tech equipment. How she resisted the urge to prank vendors on a call, we'll never know.

On a whim, Wanda decided to enter a local Coors Light Super Talent Showcase performing stand-up comedy. The audience adored her and howled with laughter. She lost the showcase, but she won something even more precious: a calling. Turns out, Wanda loved getting laughs.

For the next five years, Wanda honed her act in comedy clubs around the DC area. She found a voice and style made up of keen, insightful takes on the idiosyncrasies of everyday life, delivered through her punchy, tell-it-like-it-is, plainspoken persona. In one bit she laments the fact that, unlike men, women can't seem to shut off the constant stream of thoughts roiling through their minds. Even when women try to go to sleep at night, says Wanda, "We can't shut the hell up. You in the bed and your mind is just racing about nothing, just: *I need to talk to her tomorrow because I don't like the way she spoke to me today and I'm not going to have this uncomfortable thing going on between us did I lock the door I should have bought those shoes where's my high school yearbook what am I going to have for lunch tomorrow?* Wanda found a way to make you feel like you were hanging out with your favorite funny girlfriend: the kind of pal who could question your hair choices and your life choices with the same amount of wit and candor.

When she felt she had enough experience under her belt, she quit her NSA job and moved to New York City. Wanda's first big break came when she landed a slot opening for comedian Chris Rock at the iconic Caroline's Comedy Club. Caroline's had seen every comic hopeful from Rosie O'Donnell to Paula Poundstone grace its stages. Impressed with her act, Rock hired Wanda to write for his *Chris Rock Show*. Wanda spent five years writing and performing for the show, earning her an Emmy for Outstanding Writing for a Variety, Music or Comedy Special.

The Chris Rock Show opened the doors for Wanda to a long career in television. She took on roles in shows such as Julia Louis-Dreyfus's successful sitcom *The New Adventures of Old Christine*, *The Drew Carey Show*, *Curb Your Enthusiasm*, and, more recently, *Black-ish*. Wanda made history in 2009 when she was only the third African-American woman to host her own late-night show, *The Wanda Sykes Show*. Though the show ran for only one season, it gave Wanda an important new platform to expand her material and bring humorous and critical insights to issues related to politics, race, and, as a gay woman herself, sexuality.

As Wanda has continued to divide her time between TV and film projects and, her first love, stand-up comedy, she has become an important advocate for LGBTQ rights. In 2009 she was the first African-American woman and openly gay comedian to perform at the White House Correspondents' Association Dinner. Wanda continues to push for more diversity and representation in the comedy industry, both in terms of who is seen on camera or onstage and who makes hiring decisions in writing rooms and production teams. Though Wanda has been giving audiences her singular type of truth-in-comedy for more than three decades, her ability to keep her humor and outlook fresh and evolving, along with the complicated times, makes her seem like a bold, new comic voice just arriving to join the party.

"If you feel like there's something out there that you're supposed to be doing, if you have a passion for it, then stop wishing and just do it."

—WANDA SYKES

AFTERWORD

Thank you so much for reading this book, funny person!

I'm sorry, what's that? Why are you shaking your head? What do you mean, I'm not talking about you? Oh, I see. You're going:

Me? No. No, I mean, I'm not funny funny. My sister gave me this book because she knows how much I heart Kristen Wiig and Kate McKinnon and, yeah, I can quote Girls Trip *and* Pitch Perfect *on a dime . . . but I'm no . . . . Oh sure, I love to laugh, who doesn't? You'd have to be a zombie or a robot or a robot zombie if you don't enjoy gut-busting LOL-ing. And I have a good sense of humor. I'm not above laugh-snorting over one of those videos of Grandma twerking at someone's wedding. But I'm not, like, for-real funny, like funny-on-purpose funny.*

Yeah, I get it. Let me clear this up for you: You're wrong. If there is anything I hope you take away from this book, it's that funny is a superpower that we all have—even *you*. At one point or another, all the women in this book were just like the rest of us: regular people with a passion or geek-level love for comedy and humor in all its forms. The only difference being that each of the women in this book turned that passion for comedy into action, daring to follow the funny to see where it might take them. Maybe after reading their stories you feel compelled to do the same. Brave up and go for it! Sign up for that improv class, write a funny essay, grab your smartphone and shoot a sitcom pilot. You don't have to be a "for-real, funny-on-purpose person" to reap the comedy rewards. You just have to embrace *your* humor in whatever way you can. Find whatever it is that makes *you* laugh and share it with your friends, your coworkers, your family, and, maybe someday, the rest of the world.

FURTHER READING

Most of the amazing women profiled in this book have lots of media to share: books, biographies, videos, stand-up specials, blogs, documentaries. Dig into their materials to learn more about them and, of course, support live performance/comedic art as much as possible!

For some deeper reading on American comedy in general, the following are great additions to your physical or electronic bookshelf:

Apatow, Judd. *Sick in the Head: Conversations about Life and Comedy.* New York: Random House, 2015.

Fields, Anna. *The Girl in the Show: Three Generations of Comedy, Culture, and Feminism.* New York: Arcade Publishing, 2017.

Knoedelseder, William. *I'm Dying Up Here: Heartbreak and High Times in Stand-Up Comedy's Golden Era.* New York: PublicAffairs, 2009.

Kohen, Yael. *We Killed: The Rise of Women in American Comedy.* New York: Sarah Crichton Books, 2012.

Nachman, Gerald. *Seriously Funny: The Rebel Comedians of the 1950s and 1960s.* New York: Pantheon, 2003.

Peisner, David. *Homey Don't Play That!: The Story of In Living Color and the Black Comedy Revolution.* New York: Atria/37 Ink, 2018.

Sacks, Mike. *And Here's the Kicker: Conversations with 21 Top Humor Writers*. Ohio: Writer's Digest Books, 2009.

Scovell, Nell. *Just the Funny Parts: . . . And a Few Hard Truths about Sneaking into the Hollywood Boys' Club*. New York: Dey Street Books, 2018.

Shales, Tom, and James Andrew Miller. *Live from New York: An Uncensored History of Saturday Night Live*. Boston: Little, Brown and Co., 2002.

Stein, Ellin. *That's Not Funny, That's Sick: The National Lampoon and the Comedy Insurgents Who Captured Mainstream*. New York: W.W. Norton & Company, 2013.

Thomas, Mike. *The Second City Unscripted: Revolution and Revelation at the World-Famous Comedy Theater*. New York: Villard Books, 2009.

Wasson, Sam. *Improv Nation: How We Made Great American Art*. New York: Houghton Mifflin Harcourt Publishing, 2017.

ACKNOWLEDGMENTS

Don't let anyone fool you—this part is, without a doubt, the most stressful part of writing a book.

Giant and maybe lame, but definitely heartfelt, blanket statement to every person who has believed in me, indulged my weirdness (read: laughed at my funny bits), and encouraged and supported my writing throughout the years. It means more to me than I can ever fully express.

High fives to my family—Mike, Mom, Pat, Vanessa, Teddy, and Tim—for your inexhaustible supply of love, support, patience, and plenty of ice cream.

Endless gratitude for the family I've chosen—Christina Gillease and Mary Baum, Tom Pirozzoli and Kate Phelan, Willy Porter, Michelle Baker, Shaunda Belanger, Todd and Donna Young, Andy Aylesworth, Bishara and Michele Shbat, Kate Poppe, Julianna Reed, Cam Khalvati, Pat Furlong, Kathi Kinnon, and Nicole Polizzi-Semon. You have all inspired and challenged me and helped me to grow creatively and personally. You are also a great audience! You should have realized by now what a mistake it is to give my silliness even the smallest bit of encouragement. Foolish mortals. I love you all so much.

Lilly Ghahremani—my indomitable, rockstahh, supahhstahh (#Boston) literary "thug" agent. You have been my constant cheerleader and creative lifeline. You championed this project in its infancy and through all its growing stages and pains. You believed in me from nothing more than an email and you believe in me still. I'll never know what I did to deserve you in my corner, but I'm not going to put that under the microscope. I am eternally grateful for you and for everyone at Full Circle Literary. It's an honor and privilege to be a part of this community.

Thank you Jordana Tusman for your editorial wizardry, your patience, and your great energy and enthusiasm for this project. You made this very fun and easy. It's going to be like that for every book, right? #neverleaveme.

Thank you so much to the wonderful Anne Bentley for your beautiful, powerful illustrations, book designer Frances Soo Ping Chow, and the entire team of wonderful, creative people at Running Press and Hachette Book Group.

To my truly wonderful, small but mighty trio of writing sisters: Terri Brosius, Mary Horgan, and Karen Harris. Your support and energy has meant the world.

Many years ago, I wrapped up a PhD in Theatre and Drama from Northwestern University, just outside of Chicago, and moved home to Boston. I did the thing that so many of these phenomenal women in this book did: I stopped pressing my little face against the glass of the comedy world and I yanked open the door and ambled on in. I found an amazing, talented, richly funny community at ImprovBoston and more specifically I found the Women in Comedy Festival. Thank you to festival founders Michelle Barbera, Elyse Schuerman, and Maria Ciampa for creating a space and an event designed to amplify the voices and gifts of hundreds of funny women from all over the world. Thank you for letting me be a part of this magic and advocacy. Thank you to everyone involved in the festival past and present.

Finally, gratitude to the brave, funny women in this book, beyond, and yet to be.